A Research Guide
for Undergraduate
Students

Sixth Edition

A Research Guide for Undergraduate Students

English and American Literature

Nancy L. Baker

AND

Nancy Huling

The Modern Language Association of America
New York   2006

For information about obtaining permission to reprint material from MLA book publications, send your request by mail (see address below), e-mail (permissions@mla.org), or fax (646 458-0030).

Library of Congress Cataloging-in-Publication Data

Baker, Nancy L., 1950–
    A research guide for undergraduate students : English and American literature / Nancy L. Baker and Nancy Huling. — 6th ed.
      p. cm.
    Includes bibliographical references and index.
    ISBN-13: 978-0-87352-924-2 (pbk. : alk. paper)
    ISBN-10: 0-87352-924-3 (pbk. : alk. paper)
    1. English literature—Research—Methodology—Handbooks, manuals, etc. 2. American literature—Research—Methodology—Handbooks, manuals, etc. 3. English speaking countries—Intellectual life—Bibliography. 4. American literature—History and criticism—Bibliography. 5. English literature—History and criticism—Bibliography. I. Huling, Nancy, 1950– II. Title.
    PR56.B34 2006
    820.72—dc22   2006007360

Published by The Modern Language Association of America
26 Broadway, New York, New York 10004-1789
www.mla.org

Contents

Preface to the Sixth Edition

In 1982, when the first edition of this literary research guide was published, the microcomputer revolution was a phenomenon waiting to happen. The first edition was written on an electric typewriter. Just three years later, when the second edition was drafted, this typewriter was retired to the attic and replaced by a Kaypro personal computer with a CP/M operating system. By 1989, the Kaypro had joined the electric typewriter in the attic, and a more sophisticated Macintosh SE/30 was used to write the third edition. We wrote the fourth edition on a more powerful Macintosh, a Quadra 610. The fifth and sixth editions were typed on laptop microcomputers—an IBM Thinkpad 385ED and a Dell Latitude D600, respectively. These laptops were also used to consult many of the electronic reference sources discussed in both guides. This personal technological history in no way represents state-of-the-art developments in the greater world of automation. Nevertheless, it is symbolic, in its modest way, of an even more dramatic electronic metamorphosis undertaken by libraries during this same period.

The computer, which has reshaped so many aspects of our lives, has transformed even that most humanistic pursuit, literary research. Whereas the first edition of our guide spoke of card catalogs and printed indexes, electronic catalogs and indexes are now the norm. Although printed versions of many reference books and scholarly journals and books are still available, it is virtually impossible to get students to use them if an electronic alternative is available. We consulted many of the sources discussed in this guide from a distance, from our offices or homes, over the Internet. This method of retrieving information will increasingly become the norm.

The bewildering pace of these changes will continue to escalate. During the late 1990s, some speculated that ninety-eight percent of all new information would be created and stored in digital format by the beginning of the twenty-first century. Although this prediction may have been a bit ambitious, there is no question that more and more information is published digitally each year. From the time this book goes to press to the time it reaches you, many new electronic resources will have become available.

For this edition of *A Research Guide for Undergraduate Students: English and American Literature*, we would like to acknowledge and thank Faye Christenberry, English studies librarian at the University of Washington, for her substantive recommendations. We are equally grateful to Theresa Mudrock, history librarian at the University of Washington, for her creative insights and to the terrific reference librarians at the University of Iowa for all their assistance throughout this project. Lorena O'English, from Washington State University libraries, created the index for the fifth edition that provided a model for the index in this edition. Without the encouragement and support of our spouses, James Baker and Richard Huling, and of the Huling children, this edition would never have been completed. Charles A. Carpenter, now retired professor of English at Binghamton University, State University of New York, planted the seed that brought forth the original version of this guide. Last but hardly least, we sincerely appreciate all the assistance we received from the staff at the Modern Language Association of America but are especially grateful to David Nicholls, director of book publications, for his many worthwhile suggestions.

As the publication of a sixth edition implies, we have been gratified by the success of this modest guide for undergraduate students. We hope this little book continues to prove profitable to its readers.

Nancy L. Baker
University of Iowa
Nancy Huling
University of Washington

Introduction:
The Research Process

This brief guide to research methods in English and American literature is written for you, the undergraduate student. Most other research guides to literature are written for graduate students and advanced scholars, who have more experience with the library and who may need exhaustive lists of numerous specialized reference works. None of the other guides effectively deals with your problems as a library user.

Over thirty years of academic library experience has convinced us that your research requirements are special. Because your time and the scope of your work are both limited, you are unlikely to need many of the specialized reference sources accessible through the library. But most undergraduate students are not familiar enough with the basic tools and the organization of the library to use their research time efficiently. They often find the research process frustrating. When they cannot find what they need, they often assume it is just not available. Almost always they're wrong; they simply do not know how to locate what they want.

Keeping this difficulty in mind, you should not be surprised that this guide concentrates on the search for secondary sources, those materials that analyze and criticize an author's work. Most undergraduate literature assignments focus on one or more primary texts—the novels, poems, plays, and other works of cultural expression that you study and discuss in the classroom. Your instructor will probably ask you to provide, in your paper, an interpretation of one or more texts, engaging secondary sources as you develop your argument. Since you will need to provide evidence from the primary text to support your claims, it is important that you choose an authoritative edition as the basis for your study. Normally the instructor will select such an edition for classroom adoption. If you wish to use a different edition, you should consult your instructor. A famous work may be available in many different editions from many different publishers; it may even be found for free on the Internet. Some of these editions leave out important passages or contain errors, so your instructor's advice is important. Also, as you work with secondary sources, bear in mind the version of the text that these authors use.

Since it has grown increasingly common for undergraduates to consult primary sources, such as an author's diaries and letters or the newspapers or magazines that were available when the poem, novel, or play was written, we offer some guidance on the use of them. These sources can provide additional background information or a perspective that will be quite useful for some topics, especially as you conduct more-multidisciplinary research.

This guide stresses the thirty or so literary research tools that are most likely to be useful to you. An annotated list of about seventy is appended for further study. This guide also discusses basic research strategy. It presents a systematic way of locating important books and articles on English and American literature. Searching involves more than just a quick perusal of your library's online public access catalog or the first electronic index you might find. To be thorough, you should seek all pertinent articles and books on your subject. Then, even if many of these articles and books prove irrelevant to your topic, you can be confident that you have not overlooked any major study. Moreover, by structuring your research systematically, you can spend most of your time writing your term paper rather than searching for materials.

The research process is a fluid one. No single strategy is entirely successful for every problem. In suggesting a systematic approach to research, we do not mean to reduce a creative and interpretative process to a rigid lockstep. For some research problems, certain chapters of this guide do not apply at all. For many topics, the strategy and sources discussed in the first three chapters may provide all the assistance you need. In addition, you will find the research process is often cyclical, and it may be necessary to repeat some steps depending on your findings at a later stage. Individual problems require their own research strategies.

From this guide you should gain a basic understanding of what various types of reference sources can and cannot do; a working familiarity with the major indexes, bibliographies, and other research tools in literature; some tips on consulting electronic resources effectively; a taste of how to work with primary sources; and an idea of systematic research methods. The quality of your term papers should improve along with the efficiency and productivity of your research efforts.

CHAPTER ONE

Conducting Research in an Electronic Environment

The world of information has undergone rapid changes in the last ten years, significantly affecting how knowledge is stored and transmitted. Literary research has felt these changes. Libraries increasingly subscribe to Web-based electronic databases that provide complete texts of periodical and newspaper articles and even books. Many scholarly journals are now available on the Web to libraries through paid subscription. For example, the *JSTOR* database is an online collection of full-text back files of scholarly journals, some of which begin in the 1800s. And thousands of free Web sites exist on an array of topics.

Most literary research now begins with a series of electronic searches. Learning how to identify appropriate electronic indexes, search engines, and databases and understanding how to define the scope of your searches will enable you to survey the relevant literature on your topic and will save you time too. Some of the sources you may need to search include your library's online catalog, electronic indexes of scholarly writing, electronic databases of journal articles, or the entire Internet.

Doubtless you have used computers for much of your life—finding information for your classes, downloading and listening to music, performing calculations, writing papers, viewing movies, and chatting with friends. Despite the growth in the number of electronic sources, including literary texts, research in literature continues to rely heavily on print resources. This mixed environment of print and electronic sources creates challenges for the researcher. Although you may locate an article from a periodical or even an entire novel online, book-length critical studies, for the most part, continue to be published in paper format.

It is clearly tempting, as you sit in your residence hall or apartment, to rely only on those articles and resources that you can find in full text through your computer. There may be times when this strategy is appropriate, particularly for short, concentrated assignments. But many research projects will require a careful evaluation of the references you retrieve through your searches, and the best articles for your particular topic may be available only in print format in your library. It is important to consider quality when you weigh the rapid availability of a full-text online source against a source available only through a trip to the library.

Beyond the growing ability to find scholarly articles online, there seems to be a widespread belief that almost everything worth reading now is available for free on the Web. Indeed, a search of the Web for information on Mary Shelley's *Frankenstein* turns up more than 344,000 hits, a figure that likely increases daily. Many of the references are to pages created by students, faculty members, or librarians. These offer helpful information on Mary Shelley's life, background and contextual material on the book, and lists of critical works on *Frankenstein*. But it is often difficult to determine who put the Web page together. One personal Web site contains, besides a page devoted to Mary Shelley, the site creator's wedding pictures. This site has a number of essays written by people who may be students or who just have an interest in Shelley. There is no context for any of these essays, no information about the authors. Citing information found in these papers would be a mistake, given the uncertain authority. Anyone can put together an easily accessible Web site, and there is certainly nothing wrong with such a site. But students must be careful to evaluate the information they find. The sheer amount of information obtained in a general Web search for Mary Shelley's *Frankenstein* is daunting.

Compare the creation of a personal Web site with the scholarly publishing process. Most scholarly publications go through peer review. Two or three experts on the subject examine the manuscript of a journal article or book, providing comments and suggesting changes. They may recommend that the article or book not be published at all. Your professors may instruct you to use scholarly or academic articles and books. They usually mean that you need to find resources that have gone through the peer-review process. You will need to determine if the material you select meets these criteria.

Before you begin researching your paper, consider the resources at your disposal. The library has primary, secondary, and reference sources, including electronic databases. It also has reference librarians who can advise you on the research process and recommend search strategies and reference sources. Librarians often create Web pages that indicate the most important resources in the discipline. In addition to providing help in person and on the telephone, many libraries now offer reference assistance through instant messaging (IM) and e-mail.

Electronic databases and the World Wide Web have been a boon to student research. As universities and colleges provide remote access to full-text article databases, students can do a substantial amount of research outside the library, independent of building hours. Waiting until the last minute to research and write your paper is still not a wise idea, however, since the best source that you find through your computer at 2:00 a.m. may still be a print journal or book available only in the library. Your most important goal is to locate and use the best possible sources for your research, whether they are paper or electronic.

CHAPTER TWO

Using Library Catalogs

Searching Your Library's Catalog

An advanced undergraduate essay in literature should be informed by relevant scholarship on the topic. You have a responsibility not only to consult critical commentary on your topic but also to know whether another author has said what you want to say. You will likely conduct several searches, starting first with the library catalog, continuing with other indexes or databases, and perhaps returning to the library catalog as you discover new sources for your work.

One of the first resources you will need to master for literary research is your library's catalog of books, periodicals, and other collections available electronically or on its shelves. Although card catalogs once served this purpose, online catalogs now provide a listing of your library's holdings. These catalogs are also called online public access catalogs or integrated online catalogs. Not all look the same or have the same features. There are probably a dozen or so companies offering online catalog software suitable for college and university libraries. For example, our own universities—the University of Iowa and the University of Washington—use software from two companies, Ex Libris and Innovative Interfaces, respectively. Two libraries with online catalogs from the same company may have chosen different options and features. Some universities have designed and created their own online catalogs, although this practice has become rare. Some libraries give their catalog a catchy name. At the University of Iowa, the catalog is called *InfoHawk* in honor of the university's mascot, the Hawkeye. The University of Washington refers to its catalog as the *UW Libraries Catalog*.

Although online catalogs vary greatly, the one for the University of Washington is typical of most. When you call up the home page of the University Libraries, the first choice under Resources is UW Libraries Catalog (fig. 1). It is actually possible to begin a basic search

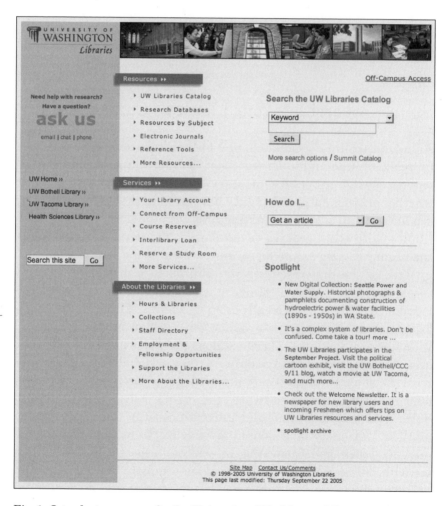

Fig. 1. Introductory screen for the *University of Washington Libraries* home page.

of the online catalog directly from this page, but for most libraries you first need to select the catalog from a menu of options. So let's click on UW Libraries Catalog.

Right from the first screen, you notice that the university has other campuses, and libraries, beyond the main Seattle one. You have the option of consulting the holdings of the entire collection (which is the default) or those of individual campuses. There are also nine different ways to search: by author, title, keyword, call number, journal, Library of Congress subject, medical subject, genre or form, and international standard book number (ISBN) (fig. 2). These searching options are fairly standard in online catalogs.

Most of the time, you will be looking for books about a particular subject, and often you will know the name of an author or the title of a book you seek. Let's assume you want to search for books of literary criticism written by Ed Folsom. To complete an author search, either pull down the menu in the By box and select Author or choose Author from the list of search options below the box. The

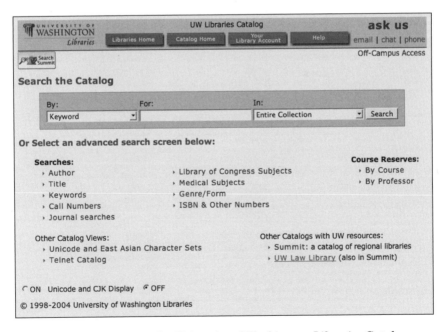

Fig. 2. Search options in the *University of Washington Libraries Catalog.*

second method gives you an author advanced-search screen with tips on how to search for authors most effectively (fig. 3). Simply type in "folsom, ed" in the box provided. Eight items match your request (fig. 4). If you select item 7, *Walt Whitman's Native Representations*, you are given a more complete bibliographic record, including place of publication, publisher, and date of publication. From the location key, you can see that the book is located in the Suzzallo/Allen Stacks (the main library at the University of Washington) at the call number provided. At the present time, no one else has checked out this book (fig. 5). The remainder of the entry lists additional bibliographic information for this title, including eight Library of Congress subject headings that reflect the content of the book. When librarians catalog a book, they assign one or more subject headings to that record, using a thesaurus of headings approved by the Library of Congress. Such headings may come in handy if you want to locate other books on the same subject. If you have a long list of items that match your search and want to create a subset of

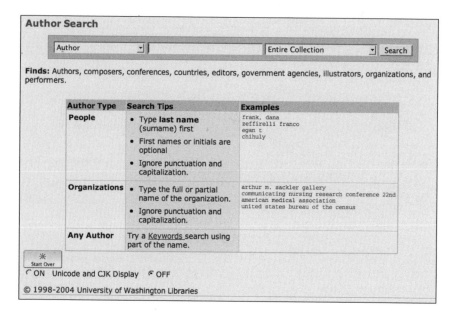

Fig. 3. Author search screen in the *University of Washington Libraries Catalog.*

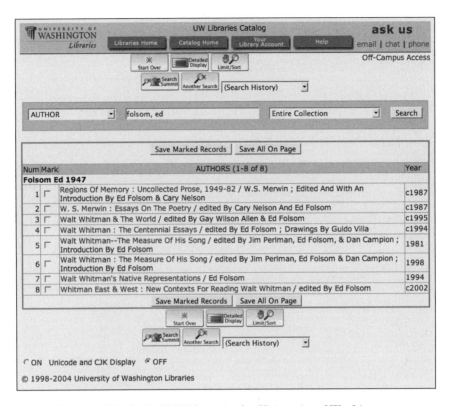

Fig. 4. Listing of books by Ed Folsom in the *University of Washington Libraries Catalog.*

those that look most useful, you can place a check mark in the box adjacent to item 7 in figure 4 and continue to browse the list, checking others that also interest you. When you have finished browsing, you can then create a shorter list of the pertinent records you have saved by selecting Save Marked Records at the top and bottom of the list.

If you select either of the boxes entitled Another Search or Start Over at the top or bottom of this screen, you can begin a different search. Another Search allows you to return to your earlier search later; Start Over does not. This ability to return could be important if you are doing a lot of searching and want to keep track of what you have already done.

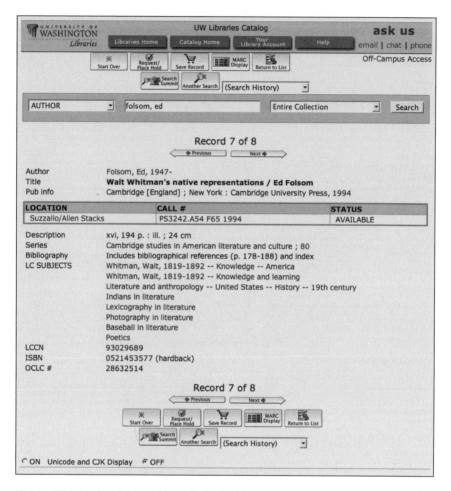

Fig. 5. The listing for Ed Folsom's *Walt Whitman's Native Representations* in the *University of Washington Libraries Catalog.*

To conduct a title search, either pull down the menu in the By box in the *Search the Catalog* screen (fig. 2) and choose Title or select Title from the list of search options below the box. As with authors, this second, advanced-search option also gives you tips on searching effectively for titles. If you are seeking a copy of the book *The Artist, Society, and Sexuality in Virginia Woolf Novels*, type the entire title or just "artist," "society," and "sexuality." You can enter a portion of the title and still retrieve the correct item because the title of this book begins with rather distinctive words for which there are no other matches (fig. 6). Otherwise you need to enter the entire title in its exact form to retrieve a match. Although author and title searches are generally straightforward, it is always advisable to try a different approach if one of them proves unsuccessful. You may have the title slightly incorrect or may have the author's name misspelled.

A thorough subject search can be more roundabout. Most online catalogs will search for keywords throughout the entire bibliographic record unless you specify which fields or which part of the record you want to search. If you are uncertain about the exact title of a book but know some of the keywords in the title, limit the keyword search to the title field to avoid retrieving a lot of irrelevant entries where the words have been used in a subject heading or other part of the record. When the author has titled the book with meaningful keywords, this kind of search can be fruitful.

Frequently you will not be looking for a book where you know the title or author. Rather, you will be seeking books relevant to a

| TITLE | ▾ | artist society and sexuality | | Entire Collection | ▾ | Search |

‹ ◆ Previous   Next ◆ ›

Author	Ronchetti, Ann
Title	**The artist, society & sexuality in Virginia Woolf's novels / Ann Ronchetti**
Pub info	New York : Routledge, 2004

Table of contents

LOCATION	CALL #	STATUS
Suzzallo/Allen Stacks	PR6045.O72 Z8669 2004	AVAILABLE

Description	xiii, 217 p. ; 24 cm
Series	Studies in major literary authors
Bibliography	Includes bibliographical references (p. 141-200) and index
LC SUBJECTS	Woolf, Virginia, 1882-1941 -- Criticism and interpretation
	Woolf, Virginia, 1882-1941 -- Political and social views
	Woolf, Virginia, 1882-1941 -- Characters -- Artists
	Woolf, Virginia, 1882-1941 -- Aesthetics
	Social values in literature
	Artists in literature
	Sex in literature
Other title	Artist, society, and sexuality in Virginia Woolf's novels
LCCN	2003027446
ISBN	0415970326 (hardcover : alk. paper)
OCLC #	53972187

Fig. 6. The listing for Ann Ronchetti's *The Artist, Society, and Sexuality in Virginia Woolf's Novels* in the *University of Washington Libraries Catalog.*

specific topic. There are several ways to conduct a subject search.
Let's begin with keyword searching. Selecting Keyword as the option,
you are given a template for listing your keyword(s). You can broaden
or narrow your search by clarifying the relation between keywords,
using connector words: "and," to limit the results to what matches
all the words you list; "or," to expand the search to include synonyms
or similar phrases; "and not," to exclude a word or concept you don't
want but will likely be included in your search results. Keywords will
search all bibliographic records unless you specify fields. For example, if you want to find books on the depiction of prostitutes in Victorian literature and you type the keywords "prostitutes and Victorian
and literature," three titles emerge that are right on target (fig. 7).
All three—*Fallenness in Victorian Women's Writing: Marry, Stitch,
Die, or Do Worse; Tainted Souls and Painted Faces: The Rhetoric of
Fallenness in Victorian Culture;* and *Walking the Victorian Streets:
Women, Representation, and the City*—were identified by searching
the entire bibliographic record. The term "Victorian" matched the
title field for each; "prostitutes" and "literature" matched the subject
headings for each (fig. 8). In this case, the ability to match keywords
throughout the bibliographic records is clearly a plus. But if you want
to find books about how childhood is portrayed in the novels of Jane
Austen and you use "Austen" *and* "childhood" in a keyword search,
you will not be entirely satisfied by the result (fig. 9). The first listing
matches "Austen" in the title field and "childhood" in the contents
field, but the book is about the juvenilia of Austen, not about how

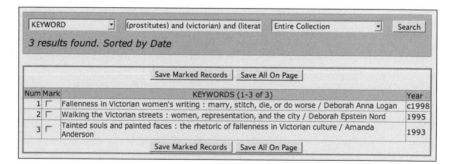

Fig. 7. The entries matching keywords "prostitutes," "Victorian," and "literature" in the *University of Washington Libraries Catalog.*

Author	Logan, Deborah Anna, 1951-
Title	**Fallenness in Victorian women's writing : marry, stitch, die, or do worse /** **Deborah Anna Logan**
Pub info	Columbia : University of Missouri Press, c1998

LOCATION	CALL #	STATUS
Suzzallo/Allen Stacks	PR115 .L64 1998	AVAILABLE

Description	x, 236 p. ; 24 cm
Bibliography	Includes bibliographical references and index
LC SUBJECTS	English literature -- Women authors -- History and criticism
	Women and literature -- Great Britain -- History -- 19th century
	English literature -- 19th century -- History and criticism
	Unmarried mothers in literature
	Moral conditions in literature
	Social problems in literature
	Prostitution in literature
	Prostitutes in literature
	Women in literature
LCCN	98006618
ISBN	0826211755 (alk. paper)
OCLC #	38765017

Fig. 8. The listing for Deborah Logan's *Fallenness in Victorian Women's Writing* in the *University of Washington Libraries Catalog.*

KEYWORD ▼	(austen) and (childhood)	Entire Collection ▼	Search

3 results found. Sorted by Date

Save Marked Records | Save All On Page

Num	Mark	KEYWORDS (1-3 of 3)	Year
1	☐	The child writer from Austen to Woolf / edited by Christine Alexander and Juliet McMaster	2005
2	☐	Rabindranath Tagore : universality and tradition / edited by Patrick Colm Hogan and Lalita Pandit	2003
3	☐	Jane Austen, the parson's daughter / Irene Collins	1998

Save Marked Records | Save All On Page

Fig. 9. The entries matching keywords "Austen" and "childhood" in the *University of Washington Libraries Catalog.*

childhood is portrayed in her novels. In the second listing, there is an essay about Austen that has nothing to do with childhood and an essay on childhood that has nothing to do with Austen (fig. 10).

Consider, for a moment, the reason for combining keywords with connectors like "and." If you seek books on madness in *Hamlet* and enter only "Hamlet," you will match over 975 entries in the *UW Libraries Catalog*, including copies of the play in print, recordings of actual performances, and books of literary criticism that contain "Hamlet" in the title, subject, or other fields. Some of these

Title	Rabindranath Tagore : universality and tradition / edited by Patrick Colm Hogan and Lalita Pandit
Pub Info	Madison, N.J. : Fairleigh Dickinson University Press ; London : Associated University Presses, 2003

LOCATION	CALL #	STATUS
Suzzallo/Allen Stacks	PK1726 .R278 2003	DUE 12-16-05

Description	297 p. ; 24 cm
Contents	Introduction: Tagore and the ambivalence of commitment / Patrick Colm Hogan -- "Nationalism is a great menace": Tagore and nationalism / Manju Radhakrishnan and Debasmita Roychowdhury -- The letters between Tagore and Noguchi, 1938 / Nobuko Yamasaki -- Contesting the boundaries between home and the world: Tagore and the construction of citizenship / Bandana Purkayastha -- Siksar Herfer: education out of whack / Kathleen M. O'Connell -- Poetic intuition and cosmic reality: Tagore as preceptor of scientific rationalism / Monish R. Chatterjee -- Consciousness and reality: the paradox of objective knowledge / Jonathan Shear -- "We think that we think clearly, but that's only because we don't think clearly": Brian Josephson on mathematics, mind, and the human world / Brian Josephson -- "Durga, for whom I would redden the earth with sacrificial offerings": mythology, nationalism, and patriarchal ambivalence in The home and the world / Kathleen Koljian -- Tabindranath Tagore's and Satyajit Ray's "new woman": writing and rewriting Bimala / Cynthia A. Leenerts -- The psychology and aesthetics of love: Srinḡara, Bh̄avan̄a, and Rasadhvani in Gora / Lalita Pandit -- Gora, Jane Austen, and the slaves of Indigo / Patrick Colm Hogan -- "Some imaginary 'real' thing": racial purity, the mutiny, and the nation in Tagore's Gora and Kipling's Kim / Jaya Mehta -- Writing across empire: W.B. Yeats and Rabindranath Tagore / Joseph Lennon -- "On the seashore of endless worlds children meet": childhood loss and mourning reaction in Tagore's poetry / Purnima Mehta -- Tagore in the Warsaw ghetto: Janusz Korczak's Post office / Judith Plotz -- Violence and creativity in the late twentieth century: Rabindranath Tagore and the problem of testimony / Ashis Nandy

Fig. 10. The listing for the book about *Rabindranath Tagore* in the *University of Washington Libraries Catalog.*

matches would be totally irrelevant with the English word *hamlet* (meaning "a small village") in the title. Had you simply requested the term "madness," you would have retrieved an equally long list of books in psychiatry and psychology along with any other titles containing the word. By linking the two keywords together, you have narrowed your result to include only items that match both words. The result is a manageable list of nine titles, one of which is clearly pertinent to your topic: *Hamlet's Enemy: Madness and Myth in* Hamlet (fig. 11). Had Theodore Lidz entitled his book instead *Hamlet's Enemy: Mental Illness and Myth in* Hamlet, your search would not have been successful, because "madness" is not in the title. Keyword searches always carry this risk. You need to think of the various synonyms the author might use and link them with "or," as in "madness or mental illness."

It increases your likelihood of conducting useful keyword searches if you use some of the other features shown in the tips section of the Advanced Keyword Search screen (fig. 12). The adjacency

KEYWORD ▾	(hamlet) and (madness)	Entire Collection ▾	Search

9 results found. Sorted by Date

| | Save Marked Records | Save All On Page | |

Num	Mark	KEYWORDS (1-9 of 9)	Year
1	☐	Separate theaters : Bethlem ("Bedlam") Hospital and the Shakespearean stage / Ken Jackson	c2005
2	☐	The new Kierkegaard / edited by Elsebet Jegstrup	c2004
3	☐	Hamlet [videorecording] / a J. Arthur Rank Enterprise, a Two Cities Films ; produced & directed by L	2000
4	☐	Evolution of consciousness : studies in polarity / edited by Shirley Sugerman ; [with contributions	c1976
5	☐	Hamlet's enemy : madness and myth in Hamlet / Theodore Lidz	1975
6	☐	Shakespeare 400; essays by American scholars on the anniversary of the poet's birth	1964
7	☐	A tribute to George Coffin Taylor; studies and essays, chiefly Elizabethan, by his students and frie	1952
8	☐	An essay on the tragedy of Hamlet. Embracing a view of Hamlet's character--his feigned or real madne	1843
9	☐	Hamlet, Prince of Denmark [videorecording] / by William Shakespeare ; [presented by] The British Bro	

| | Save Marked Records | Save All On Page | |

Fig. 11. The entries matching "Hamlet" and "madness" in the *University of Washington Libraries Catalog.*

Feature:	Search Tips:	Examples:
Adjacency	Multiple words are searched together as one phrase.	`United States supreme court`
Truncation	Words may be right-hand truncated using * (for 1-5 characters). Use ** for unlimited truncation.	`environment* polic*` `magneto**`
Operators	Use "and" or "or" to specify multiple words in any field, any order. Use "and not" to exclude words.	`(annotated bibliography) and child*` `(alaska or canada) and (adventure and not vacation)`

Fig. 12. Searching tips for advanced subject searching in the *University of Washington Libraries Catalog.*

feature can be especially useful when searching phrases. Some on-line systems will assume an "and" between words that are side by side. In this catalog, you can simply type the phrase as you would naturally, and it is searched as a phrase.

Truncation makes it easy to specify words in both singular and plural form as well as the same root of the word for which its noun, adjective, adverb, and other forms could apply. For example, the truncated form "child**" in our search on Jane Austen and child-hood would retrieve the keywords "child," "childhood," "children" along with similar derivations. Without this feature, you would need to type all these terms, with any other variations, and connect them with "or." The proximity feature provides a way to search for words that need to be near each other but not necessarily side by side or in a specified order. For example, had we used both the truncation and the proximity features in our earlier search—"austen near child*"—we would not have retrieved the irrelevant record in figure 10, but we would have retrieved a critical edition of Austen's *Mansfield Park*, which did not surface in our earlier search and might be useful for your research (fig. 13). Although these same capabilities are offered by most library catalogs, they are not always implemented in the same way. For example, some catalogs use a different symbol for truncation. Therefore it is worth paying attention to search tips that are provided and consulting the Help screens or menus until you are more familiar with a catalog's features.

You can also search for books on a specific topic by Library of Congress subject headings. As mentioned earlier, when a book is

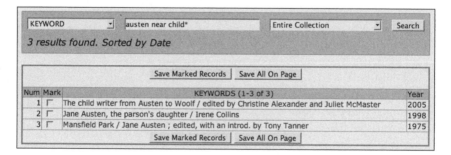

Fig. 13. The entries matching "Austen near child*" in the *University of Washington Libraries Catalog.*

cataloged, subject headings are assigned to it. *Library of Congress Subject Headings* is the official guide to these headings. Usually shelved near the reference desk, this guide does not generally list personal names. Shakespeare, the one exception to this rule, is included in the guide to demonstrate the variety of subdivisions that can be used with an author's name as appropriate. Under the heading "Shakespeare, William, 1564–1616—Bibliography," you might find a critical bibliography that could be a good starting point for your research (fig. 14). Literary criticism on specific works will be listed under the author's name and dates and the name of the work. Criticism on *Hamlet*, for example, will be found under the heading "Shakespeare, William, 1564–1616. Hamlet." An important subdivision is "Criticism and interpretation," which is often used after an author's name to identify studies concerned with more than one of the author's works. Familiarize yourself with these subdivisions. They may be used with other authors in English and American literature. Once you determine which subject headings are appropriate, choose LC Subject from the menu of search options in Advanced Keyword Search (from the home page, the path is UW Libraries

Shakespeare, William, 1564-1616.   Hamlet
— **Bibliography**
— **Concordances**
    BT   Shakespeare, William, 1564-1616—
        Concordances
— **Congresses**
— **Criticism, Textual**
    BT   Shakespeare, William, 1564-1616—
        Criticism, Textual
— **Exhibitions**
— **Illustrations**
    BT   Shakespeare, William, 1564-1616—
        Illustrations
— **Indexes**
— **Juvenile films**
— **Juvenile literature**
— **Juvenile sound recordings**
— **Pictorial works**
— **Sources**
    BT   Shakespeare, William, 1564-1616—
        Sources
Shakespeare, William, 1564-1616
— **Acting**

Fig. 14. Beginning of the section on Shakespeare in *Library of Congress Subject Headings*, 27th ed., vol. 5 (6186).

Catalog; Keywords) and type in the keywords in those headings, without punctuation.

The online catalog itself can suggest appropriate subject headings. If you return to the entry about Virginia Woolf (fig. 6), you will notice seven subject headings assigned to that book. These subject headings might lead you directly to other pertinent works on your topic. If you are particularly interested in her depiction of artists, just select "Woolf, Virginia, 1882–1941—Characters—Artists," and you will get two matches, this book by Ronchetti and another by Lisa Williams, which might be useful (fig. 15).

Notice also that *Library of Congress Subject Headings* regularly supplies the general call numbers assigned to books and other library materials on given subjects. These numbers can be helpful for browsing. Although browsing can be productive, a random exploration of the bookshelves is no substitute for a systematic search of the catalog and appropriate reference sources. Some books related to your topic may be off the shelves when you browse, or they may be classified elsewhere. Most online catalogs, like Washington's, have a browsing feature that allows you to move from one entry to others with the same general call number. You can browse online without fear of missing items that are currently in use. You can also save yourself some walking. In the *UW Libraries Catalog,* you simply need to select the call number in any bibliographic record or choose Call Numbers from the search options and type in the number for a book you know. You will find yourself in a list of library materials near that call number. If you select any call number in this list, you

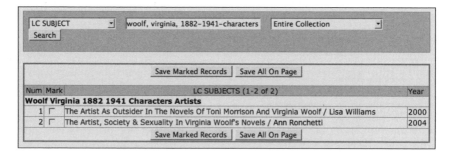

Fig. 15. The entries matching Library of Congress subject heading "Woolf, Virginia, 1882–1941—Characters—Artists" in the *University of Washington Libraries Catalog.*

will be sent to the corresponding bibliographic records and circulation status.

Speaking of circulation status, the catalog will usually tell you not only whether a book is or is not checked out but also, if the book is not yet available, when it was ordered or if it is being processed. Most libraries are willing to hasten the processing of items specifically requested by users. You can usually request, online, that a book be rushed through processing and held for you at circulation, just as you can recall a book that is circulating to another borrower. Be sure to recall items you need rather than wait for someone to return it. Some libraries have lengthy borrowing privileges, and the current borrower may even renew the book before or when it is due.

In addition to the features described above, most online catalogs have ways to limit your search by language, a specific date or range of dates, publication type, and other qualifiers. These features can be especially helpful if you are searching a large database or if your search generates a long list of matches. For example, if you are looking for recently published literary criticism, it can be helpful to limit the search by a range of dates. The publication type can help you find a film version of *Hamlet*, or it can exclude the film versions of this play from an already long list of matches.

Most of the items you find from your catalog will be books. Examine each of them to see if it is peer-reviewed. Most books published by university presses and scholarly societies fall into this category. Some commercial publishers also use peer review for quality control. If a book includes careful documentation of sources, you can tell that the author and publisher are striving to meet scholarly standards. Just as the table of contents and the index can be helpful in determining whether the book addresses your topic, the list of works cited can lead you to additional sources on your topic. Acknowledgment of an editorial board or consultants who reviewed the book for publication is also a good clue that the book has been refereed.

One additional tip on online catalogs that will be critical in the next chapter: some libraries do not catalog their journals or assign them a call number. Instead the journals are shelved alphabetically in a separate section devoted to periodicals. These journals may not be included in the online catalog but may be listed in a separate database or printed listing. Your reference librarian can tell you the method chosen by your library.

Finally, be sure to confer with your reference librarian before you finish this step in your research. Your online catalog is, quite obviously, an extremely powerful research tool, one to which you will often return as you work on your term paper. The companies that produce the software for online catalogs frequently offer new enhancements. The *UW Libraries Catalog* may have additional features by the time this book is published. Incidentally, keep track of the subject headings and keywords you find most productive. Many of them will be equally useful when you search for essays in the next chapter.

Moving beyond Your Library's Catalog

In the course of your research, you may discover that your library does not have all the books or periodicals that you want to read. As your research skills become more sophisticated, your need for materials not in your college library begins to mushroom.

Although some private colleges and universities do not open their libraries to nonaffiliated students, most academic libraries permit free use of their collections, provided that visitors do not remove any materials from the building. Some libraries in the same geographic area have even developed reciprocal borrowing privileges. Many state colleges and universities permit residents of the state to borrow books from their libraries for a small fee. Do not overlook the local public library. In some communities, particularly in large cities, the resources at the public library are more extensive than those in the local college library.

Since so many college and university libraries have made their online catalogs accessible over the Internet, you can often determine when a trip to the neighboring library will be worthwhile before you go there. Many libraries have created links on their home page to online catalogs of libraries in the state or region. Some libraries in the state or region have created group catalogs by combining the bibliographic records from their online catalogs into a single database. If your library participates in such a consortium, it may be especially easy for you to see which titles are held by other member libraries. Many of these consortia make it possible to request a book or journal article from another member library directly from the joint online catalog.

The University of Washington Libraries belong to a consortium of academic libraries in the Pacific Northwest called the Orbis Cascade Alliance. This consortium has a group catalog called *Summit*. Whenever you search the *UW Libraries Catalog*, you can search *Summit* by simply selecting the button at the top of the search screen labeled Search Summit. For example, if you are a University of Washington student looking for a book by Peter Bjork entitled *The Novels of Toni Morrison: The Search for Self and Place within the Community* and were unable to locate that book in the *UW Libraries Catalog*, you could turn to *Summit* to see if any of the other regional libraries have this book. You discover that three other libraries in the consortium have this title in their collections (fig. 16). If you select "3 Summit libraries have this item" in the middle of the screen, you can see that the University of Oregon, Washington State University, and Western Washington University have the book; you also see the call number and circulation status of each institution's copy (fig. 17).

As a student affiliated with one of the member institutions, you can request this item directly online by choosing REQUEST THIS ITEM in the middle of the screen and following the directions provided. *Summit* uses the same online software as the *UW Libraries Catalog*, so it has the same searching features. Some libraries participate in consortia using software for their group catalog that differs

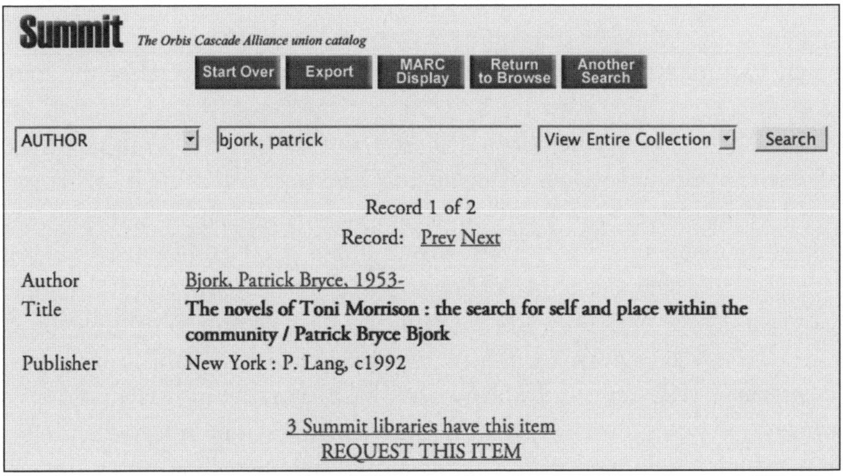

Fig. 16. Listing for book by Patrick Bjork in *Summit*.

Author	Bjork, Patrick Bryce, 1953-
Title	The novels of Toni Morrison : the search for self and place within the community / Patrick Bryce Bjork
Publisher	New York : P. Lang, c1992

HOLDINGS FOR Summit CENTRAL DATABASE
REQUEST THIS ITEM

U of Oregon	Washington State U	Western Wash U

Institution	Location	Online Access	Call Number and Holdings	Status
U of Oregon	KNIGHT		PS3563.O8749 Z56 1991	DUE 12-22-05
Washington State U	WSU Holland		PS3563.O8749 Z56 1992	AVAILABLE
Western Wash U	Wilson 3W -Books		PS3563.O8749 Z56 1991	AVAILABLE

Fig. 17. Library holdings and circulation status for book by Patrick Bjork in *Summit*.

from the software of their own catalog. Because the joint catalog may not look the same or have the same searching features as the home institution's catalog, the Help screens can be especially informative. Not all library consortia provide the circulation status in their group catalog. To check the circulation status of these, you need to consult the individual school's library catalog. Similarly, in some group catalogs it is not possible to request a copy of the item online. You would need to make the request through your library's interlibrary loan department, where your library can borrow books and periodical articles for you from other libraries. You can make such a request even if you are not sure which other library has that title. The interlibrary loan process can take time, so begin your research early if you are likely to need materials from other libraries. Familiarize yourself with library services that permit you to borrow materials from other libraries. Your reference librarian is the best person to inform you of interlibrary loan policies, of any direct borrowing capabilities of your cooperative catalog, and of any reciprocal borrowing arrangements or other privileges available at nearby libraries. The reference librarian can also help you make the most effective use of your own library catalog and any others you might need to consult.

Chapter Three

Searching Bibliographic Databases

A great deal of literary criticism appears in scholarly journals, in anthologies of critical essays, and in books written by a single author. While your library may hold these works, the individual articles will not be indexed in the library catalog. Nor will it be readily apparent from the catalog that a specific essay in a book of collected essays is exactly on your topic. Even though you may have identified some articles through a bibliography for this topic, you will need to look for others by consulting an appropriate index or database. Then you need determine whether your library owns the journals or books in which the articles are published.

There is an added benefit to searching bibliographic databases. Many of them index books as well as articles. Since your library may not own all the important books on your topic, a search of a bibliographic database will alert you to the existence of these important works as well. Your library's interlibrary loan department may be able to get them for you.

When searching for periodical articles, you should make sure that they are published in peer-reviewed or refereed journals. As noted in chapter 1, peer review means that the editors of the journals have sought the advice of experts in the field (known as peers or referees) before publishing an article. These peers—sometimes as many as three—read the article and comment on the subject matter, the strength of the argument presented, the originality, and the currency of the research. The journal editor uses these reports to decide whether or not to publish the article. Each article that appears in a peer-reviewed or refereed journal has therefore undergone intensive scrutiny. Many of the electronic databases to which your library subscribes allow you to limit your searching to peer-reviewed publications. Your reference librarian can help you use this feature and can also help you figure out what is peer-reviewed and what is not.

Where you begin your search for scholarly articles on your topic depends on the scope of your project and on the availability of material. There is likely to be limited information on an author who has become prominent in the last decade or on a topic that is just beginning to receive attention. Established authors such as William Shakespeare or Emily Dickinson have been studied endlessly, resulting in an overwhelming amount of critical material. In these cases, it can be a challenge to sift through the many resources.

Identifying and locating articles on your topic may require perseverance, whether your topic has a little or a lot written on it. Creativity is also needed as you evaluate the material you find and determine how it applies to your research. If you do not find an article precisely on your topic, you may need to think along broader or different lines, using a variety of terminology.

A good, basic starting point for researching many authors and their works is the *Literature Resource Center.* This online database of biographical information and critical literature is now available in most college and university libraries, as well as in a number of public libraries. *Literature Resource Center* includes information published in a series of reference books, which your library may also have in print form. Some of the titles in this collection are: "Contemporary Literary Criticism," "Nineteenth-Century Literary Criticism," "Poetry Criticism," and "Short Story Criticism." Through the *Literature Resource Center*, it is possible to link to selected journal articles. A similar useful resource is *Literature Online,* which is discussed at length in chapter 8.

Using the *Literature Resource Center* to locate information on Sandra Cisneros's novel *The House on Mango Street,* you would find a number of excerpts from critical essays discussing various aspects of Cisneros's book, as well as some full-text essays (fig. 18). You will need to carefully evaluate the list of resources you retrieve from this database, since its literary criticism list does contain a few general magazines and newspapers that are not peer-reviewed. If you find a pertinent article online, you can check to see if it comes from a peer-reviewed journal by consulting *Ulrich's Periodicals Directory*. The online version, called ulrichsweb.com, has a symbol in front of the name of the journal indicating that it is refereed. If you do not have access to the online version of *Ulrich's*, you can consult the print version for this information. The MLA's *Directory of Periodicals*, which is bundled with the electronic version of the *MLA*

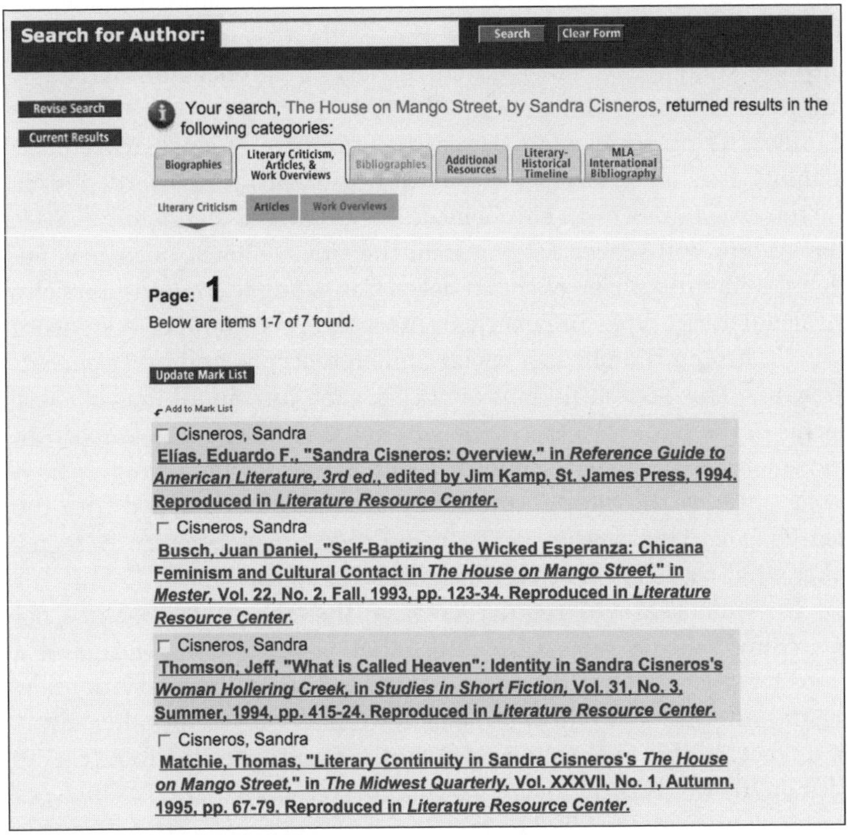

Fig. 18. Literary criticism entries for Cisneros's *House on Mango Street* from the *Literature Resource Center*.

International Bibliography, also identifies peer-reviewed journals. And of course you can consult your reference librarian.

It is likely that one resource will not provide a broad range of perspectives about a book. An excellent tool for providing such a range of articles in periodicals is the *Expanded Academic ASAP,* which covers the humanities, social sciences, and sciences. This online database contains some articles in their entirety and can be searched in a variety of ways, including by subject heading and keyword. The subject headings generally correspond to the *Library of Congress Subject Headings,* discussed in chapter 2.

When looking for a specific author and work, simply type the author's last name and part of the book title into the keyword box using the connector "and." To locate critical articles on Sandra Cisneros's *The House on Mango Street,* type the words "Cisneros" and "mango" into the search box. This search retrieves references to, and some full texts of, thirty-nine articles (fig. 19).

Identifying articles on themes in literature is much more challenging. It is generally preferable to begin with a keyword search. In the basic keyword search mode in *Expanded Academic ASAP,* the system will search for words in the titles, subject headings, authors, and summaries of the articles. For example, to locate articles on racial stereotypes in American literature, you could do a keyword search, typing the phrase "racial and stereotypes and american literature." This search finds six articles, each having all four of these terms in the title, subject, article summary, or author. It is important to remember that the computer is quite literal about language. It looks only for the words exactly as they have been typed into the search box. This search needs to be redesigned because it seems likely that there are more than six articles on the topic.

Keyword searches require creative thought. Since you are not searching specific subject headings that bring different forms of a word together under one heading, you need to find out how to allow for the singular and plural forms of a word as well as for other forms of its root. In this case, you would want to truncate to the root "rac" to pick up the words *races* and *racial* and to "stereotyp" to find *stereotypes* and *stereotypical* (fig. 20). The truncation, or wild-card, symbol for this database and many others is the asterisk. The basic keyword search

--- Citations 1 to 20 (of 39) --- ⊙ ⊙

☐ Mark all items on this page

☐ **Cisneros, Sandra. The House on Mango Street.** (Brief Article)(Young Adult
Mark Review)(Book Review) Coop Renner.
  School Library Journal July 2005 v51 i7 p44(2) (88 words)
  Text | Check UW Holdings

☐ **The House on Mango Street.** (Book Review)(Brief Review)
Mark   *Library Journal* Jan 2003 v128 i1 p192
  Citation | Check UW Holdings

☐ **Crossing gender borders: sexual relations and Chicana artistic identity.** (Critical
Mark Essay) Elizabeth Coonrod Martinez.
  MELUS Spring 2002 v27 i1 p131(19) (7172 words)
  Text | Check UW Holdings

☐ **On the "simplicity" of Sandra Cisneros's 'House on Mango Street'.** (Critical
Mark Essay) Felicia J. Cruz.
  Modern Fiction Studies Winter 2001 v47 i4 p910(33)
  Abstract | Check UW Holdings

☐ **Keeping her distance: Cisneros, Dickinson, and the politics of private**
Mark **enjoyment.** (20th-century Latina writer Sandra Cisneros, 19th-century poet
  Emiy Dickinson)(Critical Essay) Geoffrey Sanborn.
  PMLA Oct 2001 v116 i5 p1334(15)
  Abstract | Check UW Holdings

☐ **The "Dual"-ing Images of la Malinche and la Virgen de Guadalupe in**
Mark **Cisneros's The House on Mango Street.** (Critical Essay) Leslie Petty.
  MELUS Summer 2000 v25 i2 p119 (6134 words)
  Text | Check UW Holdings

☐ **Promoting adolescent voice through Latina fiction.** (Promoting Development
Mark Through Schooling, part 1) Leslie Averback.
  Child & Adolescent Social Work Journal Oct 1998 v15 i5 p379(1)
  Abstract | Check UW Holdings

Fig. 19. Entries in *Expanded Academic ASAP* matching keywords "Cisneros" and "mango."

mode in *Expanded Academic ASAP* will search for these words in the titles, subject headings, authors, and summaries of the articles. In this type of search, the use of connector words (*and, or, not*) is especially critical. The connector "and" narrows your search by limiting it to those records in which the terms so connected are found in the same reference. The connector "or," used primarily to link synonyms, broadens your search and ensures that you retrieve all citations in which at least one of the synonyms is used. Instead of using the truncation symbol for "race," we could have typed in the words "race or races or racial." You may also decide to link this group with forms of

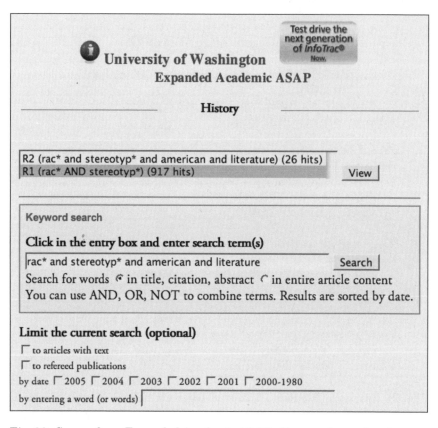

Fig. 20. Screen from *Expanded Academic ASAP* of keyword search using truncated words "rac*" and "stereotyp*" coupled with keywords "American" and "literature."

the related word *ethnic* by the connector "or," which would retrieve additional references. Some databases offer an advanced search mode that works well for combining words using both "or" and "and" in the same search.

The query of *Expanded Academic ASAP* for articles on racial stereotypes in American literature retrieves twenty-six articles that match your search. Scrolling through the list, you decide to mark a few that look relevant. From the marked list, you note the article by Kelley Blewster in *Biblio* (fig. 21) and decide to focus your attention on the works of Sherman Alexie. You can conduct a new search for

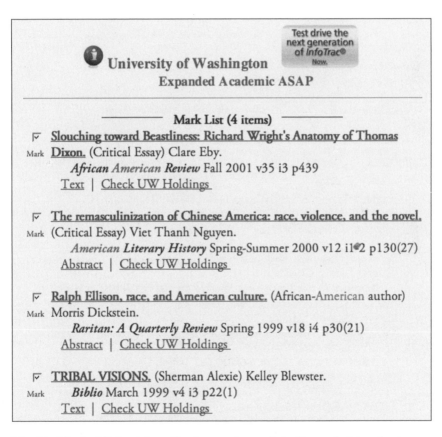

Fig. 21. Marked list retrieved by keyword search in *Expanded Academic ASAP* using truncated words "rac*" and "stereotyp*" along with keywords "American" and "literature."

pertinent articles about Alexie. Note that you can limit your search by adding words. By typing "rac*" (to include *race*, *races*, *racial*) or "ethnic*" (to include *ethnic*, *ethnicity*), you find five articles in addition to the one by Blewster (fig. 22). Scrolling to the end of one of these articles, you find links to other articles in the database on related subjects (fig. 23).

Note that in all these searches some of the references you retrieve indicate that the full text of the article is available. By choosing the

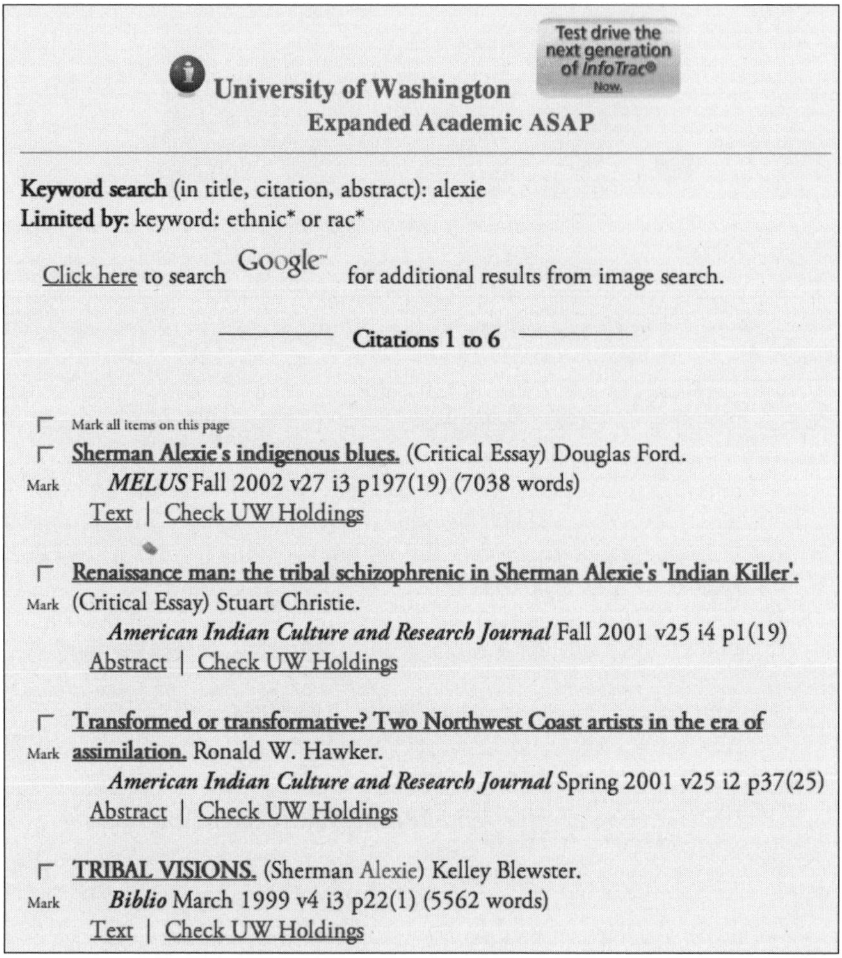

Test drive the next generation of InfoTrac® Now.

University of Washington
Expanded Academic ASAP

Keyword search (in title, citation, abstract): alexie
Limited by: keyword: ethnic* or rac*

Click here to search Google for additional results from image search.

Citations 1 to 6

Mark all items on this page

Mark **Sherman Alexie's indigenous blues.** (Critical Essay) Douglas Ford.
MELUS Fall 2002 v27 i3 p197(19) (7038 words)
Text | Check UW Holdings

Mark **Renaissance man: the tribal schizophrenic in Sherman Alexie's 'Indian Killer'.** (Critical Essay) Stuart Christie.
American Indian Culture and Research Journal Fall 2001 v25 i4 p1(19)
Abstract | Check UW Holdings

Mark **Transformed or transformative? Two Northwest Coast artists in the era of assimilation.** Ronald W. Hawker.
American Indian Culture and Research Journal Spring 2001 v25 i2 p37(25)
Abstract | Check UW Holdings

Mark **TRIBAL VISIONS.** (Sherman Alexie) Kelley Blewster.
Biblio March 1999 v4 i3 p22(1) (5562 words)
Text | Check UW Holdings

Fig. 22. The six entries matching keyword "Alexie" and truncated keywords "ethnic*" and "rac*" in *Expanded Academic ASAP*.

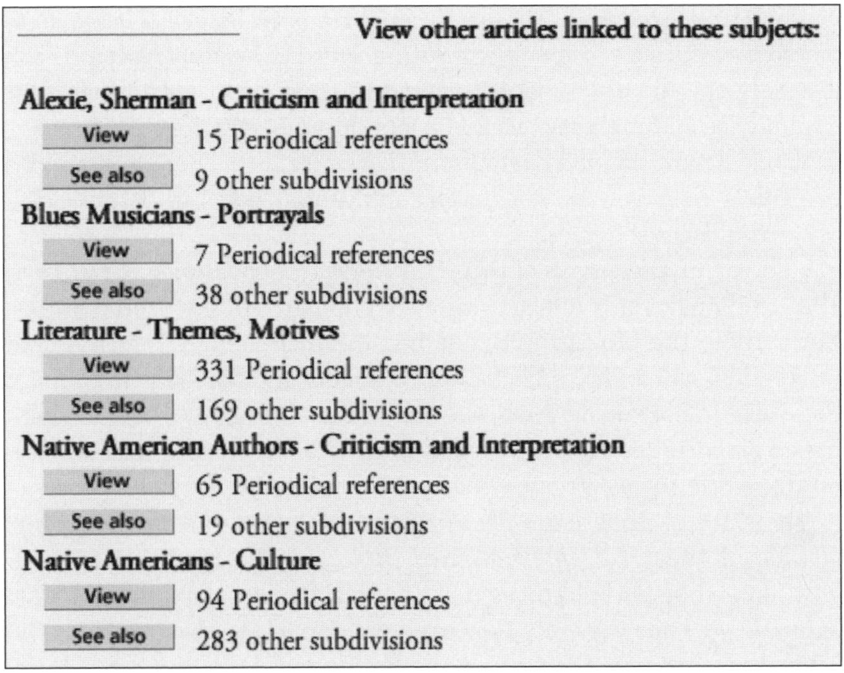

	View other articles linked to these subjects:

Alexie, Sherman - Criticism and Interpretation
    View   15 Periodical references
    See also   9 other subdivisions
Blues Musicians - Portrayals
    View   7 Periodical references
    See also   38 other subdivisions
Literature - Themes, Motives
    View   331 Periodical references
    See also   169 other subdivisions
Native American Authors - Criticism and Interpretation
    View   65 Periodical references
    See also   19 other subdivisions
Native Americans - Culture
    View   94 Periodical references
    See also   283 other subdivisions

Fig. 23. "Other articles linked to these subjects" in *Expanded Academic ASAP.*

link labeled Text (at the bottom of fig. 22), you can read the entire article. If instead of Text you see Citation or Abstract, you will need to find out whether or not your library owns the journal in which that article appears. Most libraries now provide a link in the database to either the location in the library of a print copy of the journal or a link to an online copy. Articles not carried by your library can generally be ordered through the interlibrary loan service.

If your library does not subscribe to *Expanded Academic ASAP,* other good choices for beginning your search are *ProQuest Research Library, Academic Search Premier,* and *Humanities Abstracts.*

While the *Expanded Academic ASAP* and other general databases are excellent places to begin the search for articles, they cover only a small part of the available criticism. The *MLA International Bibliography* is a much more comprehensive source; it has citations to books, articles in periodicals and books, and doctoral dissertations for the entire field of modern languages and literatures, including

English and American. (Dissertations are book-length studies completed by graduate students obtaining a PhD.) Most universities collect only the dissertations completed at their own institutions. But summaries of dissertations can be found in *Dissertations Abstracts*—or its electronic counterpart *Digital Dissertations*. These summaries can often help you by suggesting additional ways of interpreting texts and themes.

The printed volumes of the *MLA International Bibliography* from 1922 to 1955 list only literary criticism published in the United States. Since 1955, the bibliography has become increasingly international in scope; it now indexes books and periodicals published throughout the world. As of spring 2006, the electronic versions list articles published since 1926. The print format of the bibliography is issued annually, while the electronic versions are updated ten times a year.

It is likely that your library provides access to an electronic version of the *MLA International Bibliography*. Each version differs somewhat, although the basic search features are similar. Our example will use the Gale Research version (Gale also produces the *Literature Resource Center* and the *Expanded Academic ASAP*, discussed earlier in this chapter). Recall that a search of Sandra Cisneros's *The House on Mango Street* turned up thirty-nine articles in *Expanded Academic ASAP*. Perhaps only a few of those were useful to your research. Combining "Cisneros" and "mango" in the *MLA International Bibliography* search boxes finds seventy-three references in the database (fig. 24). Since the *MLA International Bibli-*

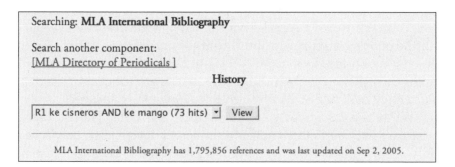

Searching: **MLA International Bibliography**

Search another component:
[MLA Directory of Periodicals]
———————————————   **History**   ———————————————

| R1 ke cisneros AND ke mango (73 hits) ▼ | View |

MLA International Bibliography has 1,795,856 references and was last updated on Sep 2, 2005.

Fig. 24. Keyword search of "Cisneros" and "mango" in the *MLA International Bibliography*.

ography includes articles in all languages, you might want to limit your search to only those languages you read. For example, by limiting your search to publications only in English, your list now has sixty-three references. Glancing through the first few references, you see that some are for articles published in books (fig. 25). One of the first references lists an article published in a book edited by an author other than the one who wrote the article (fig. 26). Neither

---

University of Washington

MLA International Bibliography

Test drive the
next generation
of *InfoTrac®*
Now.

R1 (ke cisneros AND ke mango) and la ("English")

─────── **Citations 1 to 20 (of 63)** ─────── ⊳ ⊳|

☐ Mark all items on this page

☐ **Sandra Cisneros: Crossing Borders.** McCay, Mary A. pp. 305-21.. Bak, Hans
Mark (ed.).. Uneasy Alliance: Twentieth-Century American Literature, Culture and
Biography.. Costerus: Essays in English˙ and American Language and Literature.
150. Amsterdam, Netherlands: Rodopi, 2004. 367 pp. (Book article)
[Subject Terms: American literature; 1900-1999; Cisneros, Sandra (1954-): My
Wicked Wicked Ways (1987); The House on Mango Street (1983); Woman
Hollering Creek (1991); poetry; treatment of boundary; Mexican American
experience.]
Citation | Check UW Holdings

☐ **Rhetorizing the Contact Zone: Multicultural Texts in Writing Classrooms.** Grobman,
Mark Laurie. pp. 256-85.. Schweickart, Patrocinio P. (ed. and introd.) Flynn, Elizabeth A. (ed.
and introd.).. Reading Sites: Social Difference and Reader Response.. New York, NY:
Modern Language Association of America, 2004. vii, 357 pp. (Book article)
[Subject Terms: American literature; 1900-1999; Cisneros, Sandra (1954-): The House on
Mango Street (1983); novel; relationship to multiculturalism; rhetoric and composition;
theories of Pratt, Mary Louise (1948-); "Arts of the Contact Zone". Rhetoric and
composition; teaching approaches; role of Cisneros, Sandra (1954-); The House on Mango
Street (1983); relationship to multiculturalism; theories of Pratt, Mary Louise (1948-);
"Arts of the Contact Zone".]
Citation | Check UW Holdings

Fig. 25. Listing for articles published in books matching the keyword search "Cisneros" and "mango" in the *MLA International Bibliography*.

the author, Mary McCay, nor the title of the article, "Sandra Cisneros: Crossing Borders," is likely to be listed in your library's catalog. You will need to look up the editor of the book, Hans Bak, or the title of the book, *Uneasy Alliance: Twentieth-Century American Literature, Culture and Biography*, in that catalog. The indexing of essays in books is a unique feature of the *MLA International Bibliography*, providing an excellent way to locate criticism.

The *MLA International Bibliography* currently does not provide summaries of the articles listed. Some of the full text of journals

---

McCay, Mary A. "Sandra Cisneros: Crossing Borders," pp. 305-21. Bak, Hans (ed.). Uneasy Alliance: Twentieth-Century American Literature, Culture and Biography. Amsterdam, Netherlands: Rodopi, 2004. 367 pp.

Subject Terms:	American literature; 1900-1999; Cisneros, Sandra (1954-): My Wicked Wicked Ways (1987); The House on Mango Street (1983); Woman Hollering Creek (1991); poetry; treatment of boundary; Mexican American experience.
Language:	English
Document Type:	Book article
ISSN:	0165-9618
ISBN:	90-420-1611-6
Series/Collection:	Costerus: Essays in English and American Language and Literature. 150
MLA Update:	200403
MLA Sequence:	2004-1-13865
MLA Record Number:	2004531611
Source Database:	© *MLA International Bibliography*. New York: Modern Language Association of America, 1963- .

Fig. 26. Citation for an article from a book matching a search for "Cisneros" and "mango," limited to those in the English language, from the *MLA International Bibliography*.

you need may be available electronically from your library, either through the bibliography or the library's catalog, but many will be in print format only. Another helpful feature of the *MLA International Bibliography* is the Subject Guide or Thesaurus (the name depends on the version you are using), which is a list of the subject headings used in the database. Searching the subject headings allows you to refine your search, since the headings are assigned according to the primary topics covered by the article. For example, a Subject Guide search on *The House on Mango Street* finds fifty-five articles.

As with most databases, the *MLA International Bibliography* allows you to e-mail the search results to yourself. It is always a good idea to take advantage of the Help option to learn how best to search the database, especially since features are updated and improved on a regular basis.

For online articles in older journals, an excellent resource is *JSTOR*. This database includes issues of major scholarly journals in many disciplines. The most current issues are generally between two and five years old, so *JSTOR* will not be a good source for new articles. But the archive spans many years, as far back as the 1800s. A search for articles on Cisneros's *The House on Mango Street*, first published in 1988, reveals sixty-six articles in the *JSTOR* journal collection (fig. 27). Some

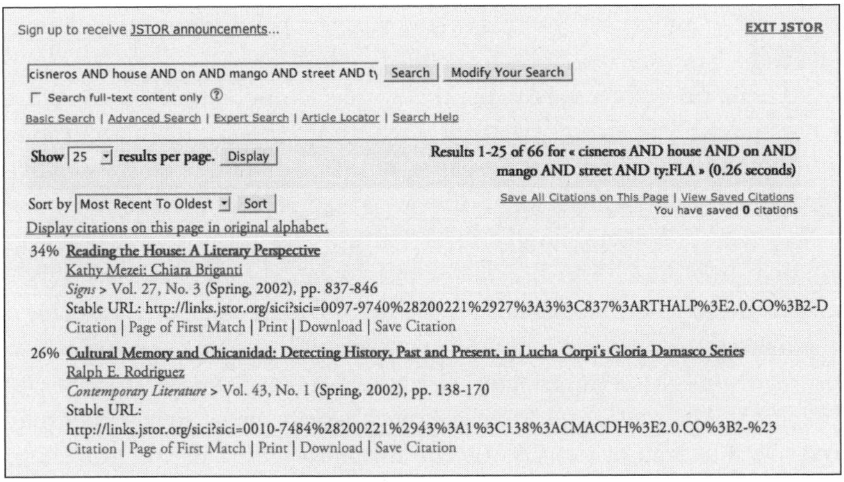

Fig. 27. Listing of results from a search in *JSTOR* combining "Cisneros" and "House on Mango Street," limited to articles.

of these articles only touch on the novel; others are in-depth discussions. The most recent article was published in 2002, so you will still need to use sources such as *Expanded Academic ASAP* and the *MLA International Bibliography* to find the current criticism. You could also use *Project MUSE* for more recently published online articles, since it covers current issues of a highly selective group of prestigious, peer-reviewed journals. In fact, *Project MUSE* has a partnership with *JSTOR*. If your library subscribes to both, you can do a single search in *Project MUSE* and it will retrieve both the recent articles (from *Project MUSE*) and the older articles (from *JSTOR*) for any titles they have in common. However, since *JSTOR* indexes more titles than *Project MUSE*, you will not want to limit your search just to *Project MUSE*. A search for criticism on *The House on Mango Street* in *Project MUSE* identified only twenty-four matches, compared with the sixty-six in *JSTOR*.

Searching electronic indexes is normally faster and more efficient than using a printed source. The ability to link together a number of keywords or to combine keywords with subject headings focuses the search in a way that is simply not possible with printed indexes, which permit you to look up only one term at a time. Electronic indexes also allow you to search many years at once instead of one year at a time. If your library does not subscribe to the electronic indexes discussed here, be sure to ask your reference librarian to recommend suitable alternatives. If you need older articles and find nothing in the *JSTOR* collection, you may need to use a print index, since many electronic indexes begin with the early 1980s.

There are other useful print and electronic resources covering English and American literature, including the *Annual Bibliography of English and American Literature*, which is available electronically. Your library may subscribe to these instead of or in addition to other resources. The increasingly interdisciplinary nature of studies in English and American literature may require that you seek scholarly articles in other disciplines such as art, history, or psychology. For example, an examination of racial and ethnic issues in American literature might benefit from a search of the sociology database *Sociological Abstracts*, and any topic with psychological overtones may require a search of *PsycINFO*, the database of article references in psychology.

CHAPTER FOUR

Searching the Web

What kind of literary information can you expect to find when conducting a general search of the Web using a search engine such as *Google* or *Alta Vista*? Fans of various authors have created Web sites, some of them quite large, on which they post a wide array of material, primarily nonscholarly in nature. Going back to our search on Mary Shelley, we also find outlines for college courses, bibliographies of criticism posted by librarians, and information about movie versions of *Frankenstein*. Digging through all these sites for criticism on Shelley would not be an effective use of time, given the large body of criticism easily found by searching some of the standard databases listed later in this book. But a general Web search for a contemporary author may be worthwhile. For example, a search for information on Sherman Alexie finds the "official Sherman Alexie" site at www.fallsapart.com. This site contains a biography, a bibliography of Alexie's works with links to tables of contents, an "academic center" listing criticism, and more.

If you decide to explore the Web extensively for literary sites, it is a good idea to consult the Help screens of the search engines you use to learn about their advanced features. Many search engines, although not as sophisticated as electronic databases offered through libraries, do permit the use of connector words such as "and" and "or." It is important to note that no single search engine scans and returns results from the entire Web. Recently, *Google* introduced a search service called *Google Scholar,* designed to help researchers find scholarly literature. You might find this feature useful as a starting point. But the number of references is much less than what you would find by doing a good search of your library's catalog and literature databases. *Google* notes that the number of full-text articles and books freely available online is limited.

Web search engines are generally not the most effective method for finding quality sites related to literature. A recent search found over 93,800 sites mentioning Sherman Alexie (compared to 1,700 sites in 1999). Even when the search engine returns the results ranked by relevance, you will still need to examine a considerable amount of information. A better strategy for finding Web sites related to the study of literature is to check the Web sites of your library and your English department. The librarian responsible for developing the collection in English and American literature has likely put together a Web page that provides links to well-organized and authoritative sites. For example, the English studies librarian at the University of Iowa maintains an extensive page that lists recommended databases for finding articles, biographical information, primary texts, and links to major literary sites (fig. 28). English departments have similar lists, and individual faculty members often create sites focusing on their specialties, such as the Victorian period or medieval literature. Highly regarded Web sites are Jack Lynch's *Literary Resources on the Net* (andromeda.rutgers.edu/~jlynch/Lit/) and Alan Liu's *Voice of the Shuttle* (vos.ucsb.edu/), both maintained by faculty members. In his *Literary Research Guide,* James Harner notes that these are "sites that offer a judicious selection of current guides to specific Internet resources" (73; see app., sec. 1). Remember that Web site addresses may change, so saving these sites through the Bookmarks or Favorites function on your computer will help you stay current.

Your evaluation of sources uncovered during a search of the Web is critical. Ask yourself questions: Who is the author? What is the context? Has the site been updated recently? Can the information be verified elsewhere? What is the value of the information found on the site compared with the range of information on the topic? How does the site compare with other sources? (Actually, these same questions can help you evaluate all the information sources, electronic and printed, discussed throughout this book.) You will want to make sure that what you use and cite in support of your research is valid and appropriate for your level of work and not merely a paper posted to the Web by a third grader who may have obtained much of the information from an encyclopedia (this has happened!). In the appendix are references to sources that will help you evaluate Web sites.

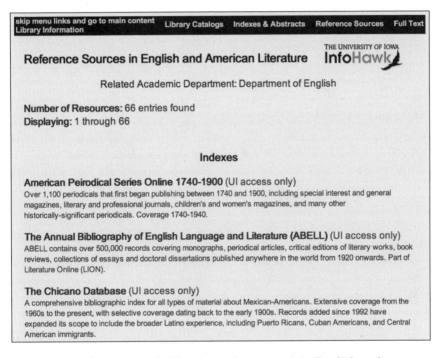

Fig. 28. List of recommended databases for research in English and American literature from the University of Iowa Libraries Web page.

CHAPTER FIVE

Finding Reviews

There may not be much criticism on a recent book, film, or drama performance; the only treatment of such a work may be a review in a current (perhaps even popular) periodical or newspaper. Book reviews are usually written shortly after a book is published and discuss it as a whole, from the perspective of whether it is worth reading or acquiring. They appear in magazines, newspapers, and scholarly journals for the specific purpose of keeping their readers up-to-date on books likely to be of interest to them. Similarly, performance and film reviews follow openings and help audiences decide what to attend. In some of your classes, you may study a book and then view a film or see a dramatic performance resulting from that book. Reviews of the film or performance may discuss how the medium interpreted it.

Criticism, unlike reviews, is usually written some period of time after the work is made public, even hundreds of years later. Critical books or articles often focus on specific aspects or themes in a book, film, or dramatic performance. An example would be a book discussing the depiction of children in a particular novel or novels by Charles Dickens or how an author uses a certain image in a novel or poem. While authors of reviews sometimes mention other works by the same author or compare the work with another, such references are certainly not a requirement for a good review. Criticism, on the other hand, will frequently compare several works in terms of a specific subject or stylistic feature. In the absence of criticism, a review may be helpful. To find reviews of books, films, and dramatic performances, you can consult some of the general databases discussed in chapter 3, as well as specialized indexes or databases that list only reviews. Some of these are listed in the appendix.

ProQuest Research Library, which was briefly mentioned in chapter 3, is an excellent example of a database that can lead you to reviews in a wide variety of scholarly and general periodicals and newspapers. Let's say you are interested in finding criticism on Cisneros's novel *Caramelo; or, Pure Cuento* (2002). A search of the *MLA International Bibliography* turns up no criticism, so you will need to rely on reviews to find out what critics think about the book. The *ProQuest Research Library* database makes it easy to search for book reviews. Using the advanced search feature, combine "caramelo" with the document type "Book review" (fig. 29). Note that the drop-down box on the right of the search boxes offers a number of options, allowing you to select where in a citation you want the search to find

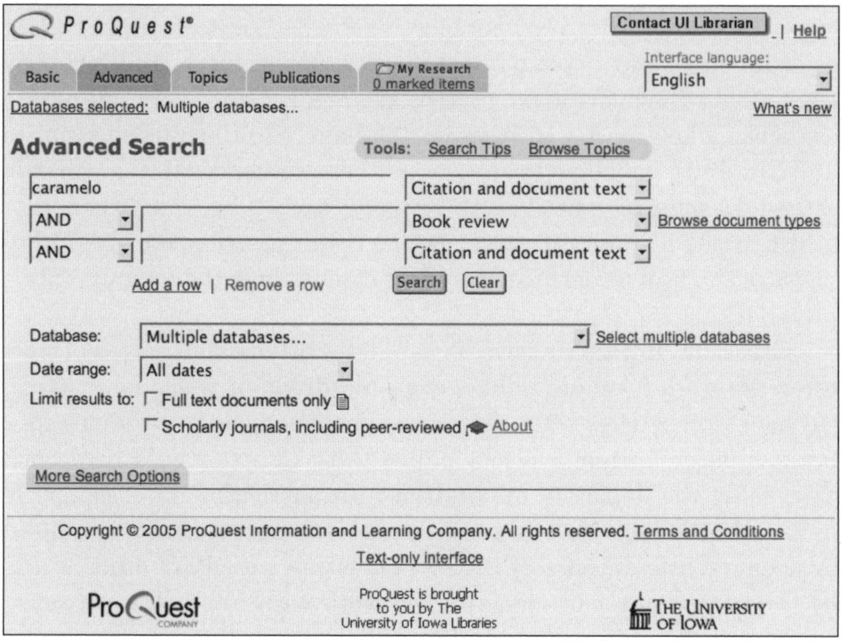

Fig. 29. Search for book reviews of Sandra Cisneros's *Caramelo* in the *ProQuest Research Library.*

your words. For reviews, we select the document-type option and can then browse and select the document type we want by clicking on the Add to Search link next to "Book review" (fig. 30). This search finds thirty-seven reviews of *Caramelo*. Note that you can view the full text for many of them (fig. 31).

If your library does not offer access to *ProQuest Research Library,* you can check databases such as *Expanded Academic ASAP, Humanities Index,* or *Academic Search Premier.* In addition, your library might have the two major indexes to book reviews—*Book Review Digest* and *Book Review Index*—in print or electronic format. For film reviews, check the *Film Literature Index* (print and online) and the *FIAF International Filmarchive Database.*

Databases and indexes listing reviews of novels also compile reviews of nonfiction. These commentaries can indicate how a book of criticism was received at the time of its publication. Assume you

Review	Add to Search
Advertising review	Add to Search
Document review	Add to Search
Arts/exhibits review	Add to Search
Audio review	Add to Search
Book review	Add to Search
Comedy review	Add to Search
Dance review	Add to Search
Film review	Add to Search
Journal review	Add to Search
Multimedia review	Add to Search
Music review	Add to Search
Opera review	Add to Search
Performance review	Add to Search

Fig. 30. List of document types that can be used to limit the search in the *ProQuest Research Library.*

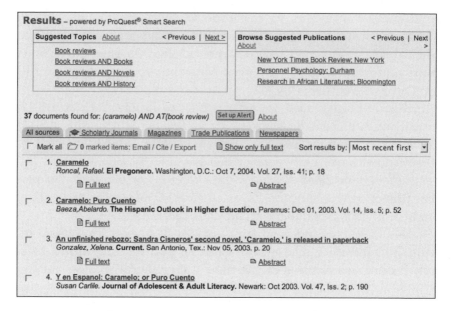

Fig. 31. Listing of entries for book reviews of *Caramelo* in the *ProQuest Research Library*; those marked "Full text" provide the entire book review online.

are preparing a paper on gender in Shakespeare and were planning to use Linda Bamber's *Comic Women, Tragic Men: A Study of Gender and Genre in Shakespeare* (Stanford UP, 1982). You might want to read reviews of this study to learn what other Shakespearean scholars think of it. While *ProQuest Research Library, Expanded Academic ASAP, Book Review Index,* and *Book Review Digest* can provide some citations, two other indexes might be better suited to this kind of research problem. *An Index to Book Reviews in the Humanities,* because it indexes reviews from over seven hundred scholarly journals, is far more likely to pick up erudite evaluations of serious studies like Bamber's. Since this index ceased publication with the 1990 volume, however, it will prove useful only if the critical work was published between 1960 and 1990. A second choice is the *Annual Bibliography of English Language and Literature*, which includes scholarly reviews.

You may be asked to compare reviews written when a book was published with the criticism that came later. How was the book originally received, and how do the initial reactions compare with the interpretations of later critics? To locate contemporary reviews of older works, check the *Combined Retrospective Index to Book Reviews in Humanities Journals, 1802–1974*. For example, you might want to find a review of Mary Shelley's *Frankenstein* written at the time the book was published. The *Combined Retrospective Index* finds that a review appeared in the *Quarterly Review of Literature*, volume 18, 1818, shortly after the book appeared. Another excellent source for finding early book reviews is the *Nineteenth-Century Masterfile*, an electronic resource, or its print counterpart, *Poole's Index to Periodical Literature*.

CHAPTER SIX

Using Contextual Primary Sources

> Moreover, no one writes in a vacuum. Whatever private
> influences are involved, authors, whether conformists or
> rebels, are the products of time and place, their mental
> set fatefully determined by the social and cultural
> environment. To understand a book, we must also
> understand the manifold socially derived attitudes—the
> morality, the myths, the assumptions, the biases—that it
> reflects or embraces.
> —Richard D. Altick and John J. Fenstermaker,
> *The Art of Literary Research*

For much of the work you undertake as a student of English or American literature, finding secondary books and articles will be sufficient for your research. But some classes may require you to look into primary sources, those documents written during the time period that you are studying, as a way of putting in context a piece or theme of literature.

Primary sources in literature consist of the work of literature itself as well as the author's diaries, journals, letters, manuscripts, and autobiography. What a writer reveals in an autobiography or diary may help you understand the themes of a particular novel, poem, or short story. Beyond these more obvious resources lies a wealth of additional primary sources reflecting the time during which the author lived. In the past, these sources may have been available only to a few scholars who could travel to the great libraries in England or the United States to do research in the collections. Through the wonders of microform and digital reproduction, many important collections can be perused at libraries throughout the country, and increasingly on your computer. There are now a number of digital primary-source collections available through the Web—many free of charge. Examples of major digital collections are the Library of Congress's American Memory Project, the *Making of America* (a collaborative project of Cornell University and the University of Michigan), the University of Virginia Library's Electronic Text Center, and Brown University's *The Victorian Web* (literature, history, and culture in the age of Victoria). Other important digital collections have been produced by commercial publishers. Your library may subscribe to some of these resources. Examples are *Early English Books Online (EEBO)* and newspapers, such as the *New York Times* and the *Times* (London).

Types of primary sources that might help you place a work or literary theme in its cultural and social context are newspaper and periodical articles published during the time period; the diaries, journals, and correspondence of those living then; and congressional and parliamentary debates. Identifying appropriate primary sources is a challenge and requires a variety of research techniques. A few of these are illustrated through the following example.

Reading Charles Dickens's novel *Oliver Twist*, published first in a periodical in 1838–39, you wonder about the lives and treatment of city children in Britain during the nineteenth century. Checking your library catalog using the keywords "children and England and history and nineteenth century," you find a book by Eric Hopkins called *Childhood Transformed: Working-Class Children in Nineteenth-Century England*. Another book found in this search is Pamela Horn's *The Victorian Town Child*, which specifically addresses the social conditions of city children. These two secondary sources provide contextual information and include bibliographies that identify the primary sources consulted by the authors.

One key to finding primary sources through the catalog is to combine major subject headings with the word *sources*, which will find collections of primary sources. An example of a book found in the University of Washington Libraries under the subject heading

"Children—Great Britain—History—Sources" is Irina Strickland's *The Voices of Children, 1700–1914* (fig. 32). Arranged chronologically, this book contains excerpts of original writings that touch on all aspects of the lives of children, including employment and living conditions. Not all libraries use the word *sources*, and it is possible to find primary sources either in collections or as individual publications through standard subject searching. To find the letters of an individual, combine the word "correspondence" with the name. In the *UW Libraries Catalog*, a search using the subject heading "Dickens, Charles, 1812–1870–Correspondence" lists such books as *Selected Letters of Charles Dickens,* edited and arranged by David Pariossien. A collection of Dickens's letters may provide further information about his views on the treatment of children.

Looking at the bibliography in Hopkins's *Childhood Transformed* indicates that Hopkins used a number of government publications when he wrote his book. In addition to checking the documents he cites, you could consult British parliamentary debates and sessional papers for further information on the treatment of children during the nineteenth century. Check your library's catalog by keyword or author to find such references as *Parliamentary Debates* (generally

| TITLE ▾ | voices of children | Entire Collection ▾ | Search |

⟨ ◆ Previous ⟩ ⟨ Next ◆ ⟩

Author	Stickland, Irina
Title	**The voices of children, 1700-1914**
Pub info	Oxford, Blackwell [c1973]

LOCATION	CALL #	STATUS
Suzzallo/Allen Stacks	HQ792.G7 S85	AVAILABLE

Description	224 p. illus. 22 cm
LC SUBJECTS	Children -- Great Britain -- History -- Sources
	Great Britain -- Social conditions -- Sources
LCCN	74164462 //r85
ISBN	0631117806
OCLC #	915369
Grsn	00549922

⟨ ◆ Previous ⟩ ⟨ Next ◆ ⟩

Fig. 32. Entry for Irina Strickland's *The Voices of Children, 1700–1914*, retrieved by performing a subject heading search on "Children—Great Britain —History—Sources" using the *University of Washington Libraries Catalog.*

cited as *Hansard's Parliamentary Debates*) and *Subject Catalogue of the House of Commons Parliamentary Papers, 1801–1900*. Because the indexes to British official publications changed names several times during the course of the century, ask your reference librarian to assist you in finding the years you need.

Primary information can also be found by using guides and indexes to the periodicals and newspapers of the day. *Poole's Index to Periodical Literature, 1802–1907* is an index by subject to articles published in some of the leading magazines of the time and can be consulted for topics related to the United Kingdom and the United States. *Poole's*, along with other indexes to periodicals and government publications, is included in an electronic database called *Nineteenth-Century Masterfile*. *The Wellesley Index to Victorian Periodicals, 1824–1900* is organized by the title of the periodical and lists the contents for each issue. There is no subject index in the print version, but you can quickly scan the listings for the years in which you are interested. For example, the contents for the September 1836 issue of the *Quarterly Review* include an article called "Glances at Life in City and Suburb," which would provide some background on general life around the time that Dickens wrote *Oliver Twist* (fig. 33). The electronic version of *Wellesley* can be searched by keywords. Yet another source to check for information on children during the time of Dickens is the *Times* (London) newspaper. *Palmer's Index to the* Times *(London), 1790–1905* covers the nineteenth century, but your library may subscribe to the electronic full-text version, called *The Times Digital Archive, 1785–1985*. Finally, an excellent primary source that is available on the Web and free is *The Victorian Web*. This site was created and is maintained by George P. Landow, professor of English and art history at Brown University, assisted by a few other scholars. Here you will find a number of references to the work and thought of Charles Dickens, along with some full-text resources (fig. 34).

Remember, when using the indexes to primary-source material, that the terminology used during the period you are studying may

---

510 *Glances at Life in City and Suburb*,
223–229. **J. G. Lockhart.** Murray.

Fig. 33. Entry 510 from *The Wellesley Index to Victorian Periodicals, 1824–1900* (718).

not match what is used today. And to improve the results of your searches, be sure to try synonyms or terms related to your topic. For example, in addition to searching for "treatment of children," you might try the phrase "care of."

So far we have focused on primary sources related to Great Britain in the nineteenth century. This same research process can be used for other periods and for the United States. If you were interested in finding primary sources related to issues raised in Upton Sinclair's *The Jungle*, published in 1906, you would want to check United States congressional publications such as hearings and laws. To find out what might be written on the meatpacking industry and on the condition of factories, consult either the print *New York Times Index* or the digital full-text *New York Times* and the print or electronic *Reader's Guide to Periodical Literature*.

Primary sources bring the period you are studying alive and allow you to develop your own interpretation in relation to the work or works you are reading rather than rely completely on secondary

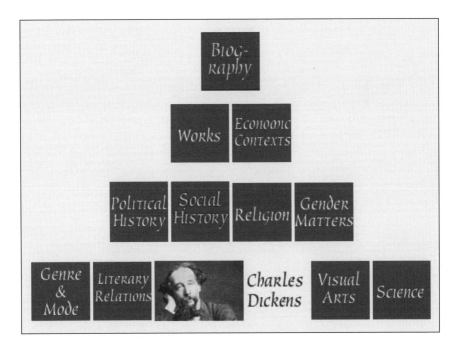

Fig. 34. Page showing author search for "Charles Dickens" in *The Victorian Web*.

material. Identifying and tracking down primary sources can be a challenge. Doubtless this task will be facilitated over time by the continued digitization of major primary documents and finding aids and their accessibility through the Web. It is important to remember, however, that sometimes pieces of text are pulled out of context and that you may still need to use printed resources to find a source in its entirety.

CHAPTER SEVEN

Finding Supplementary Information: Other Reference Sources

Biographical Sources

For most undergraduate term papers, you may not need biographical information on the authors studied in the course or on the critics who wrote about them. But occasionally a few biographical facts can shed additional light on an author's work or on a research problem. Many reference works discuss the lives of English and American writers. Some supply only a brief paragraph or two of basic data—dates and places of birth and death, major works, and the like. Others offer lengthy treatments of each author's life along with a discussion of that author's literary accomplishments.

The Dictionary of Literary Biography (DLB) is an excellent example of a comprehensive literary dictionary that provides both factual information and critical opinion. The online version consists of 11,500 biographical, bibliographic, and critical essays on North American novelists, dramatist, poets, essayists, critics, historians, journalists, and biographers. The database is drawn from the four-hundred volume printed reference source by the same name and is updated quarterly.

If your library subscribes to the *DLB* and other literary databases from the same publisher, Thomson Gale, you may be able to search them under the umbrella of *Gale Literary Databases.* As you can see in figure 35, this library offers both the *DLB* and a bio-bibliographic database called *Contemporary Authors (CA)*; the two together cover 110,000 modern authors. The information in *CA* is also derived from a printed set of reference books by the same name. You can search the *DLB* and *CA* at the same time, or you can select either database and search it separately. To locate information on the nineteenth-century novelist George Eliot, you would probably just search the *Dictionary of Literary Biography.* Simply type "George Eliot" in the box labeled Author Name. Notice that you need not capitalize the first letter of her first or last name (fig. 35). You can also search by a variety of other terms, such as title of work, or by a combination of them. Eliot published in several different literary genres, so there are three different entries in the database that match your search (fig. 36). Because this database was created from

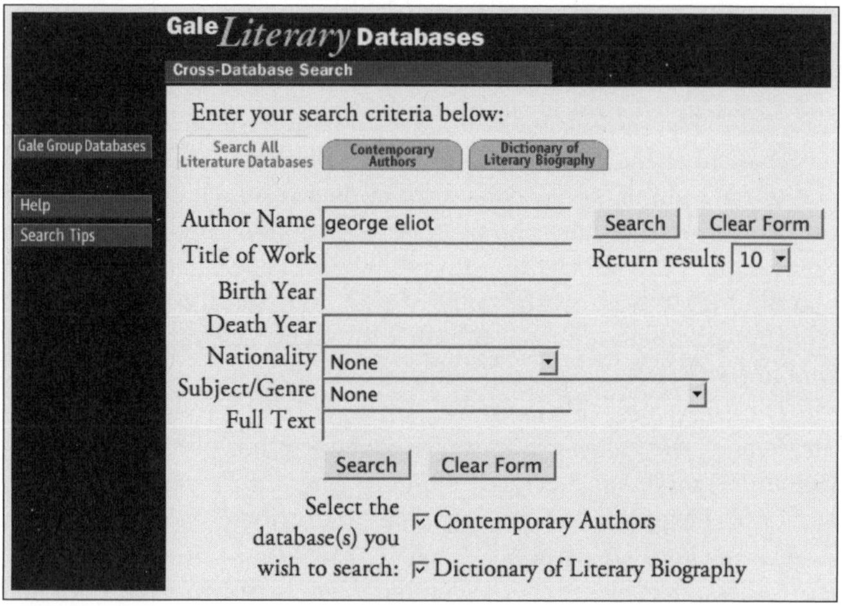

Fig. 35. Author search for "George Eliot" in *Gale Literary Databases.*

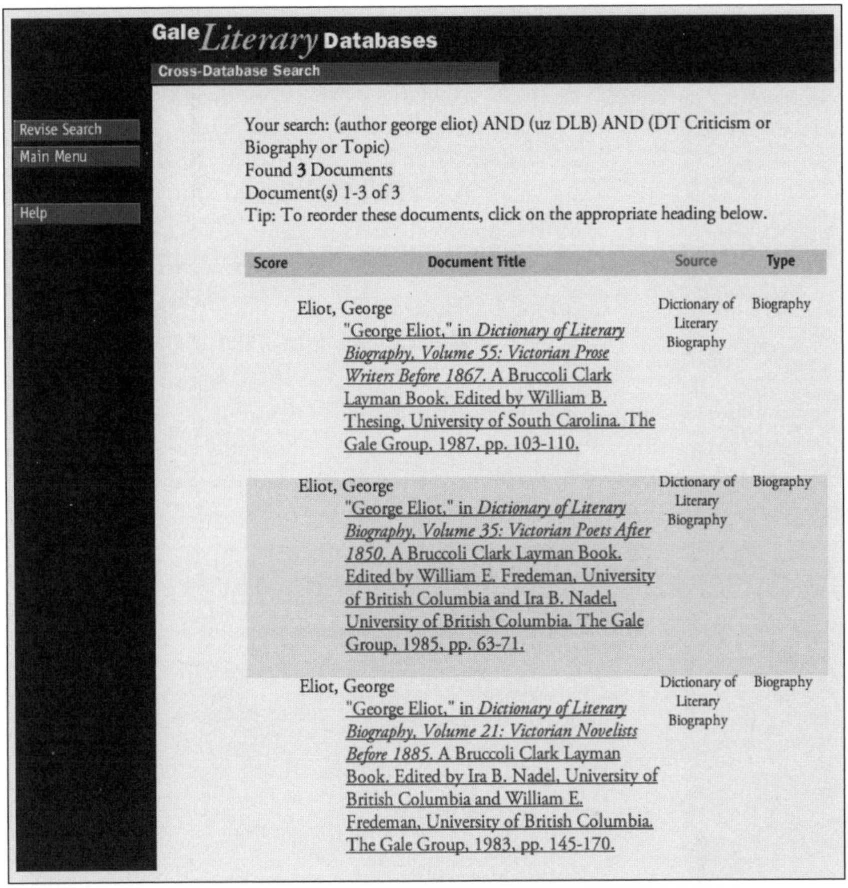

Fig. 36. Results matching "George Eliot" in *Gale Literary Databases*.

a printed reference set where authors of different genres were discussed in separate volumes, so there are three entries for the same author. Since you are specifically interested in Eliot as a novelist, select the third choice. There are a brief biographical profile and a lengthy biographical and critical essay that includes a discussion of each of her novels (fig. 37). You will also find a bibliography of works by Eliot as well as selected readings about this author. The name and institutional affiliation of the scholar who supplied this information and analysis are noted at the end. As with all databases,

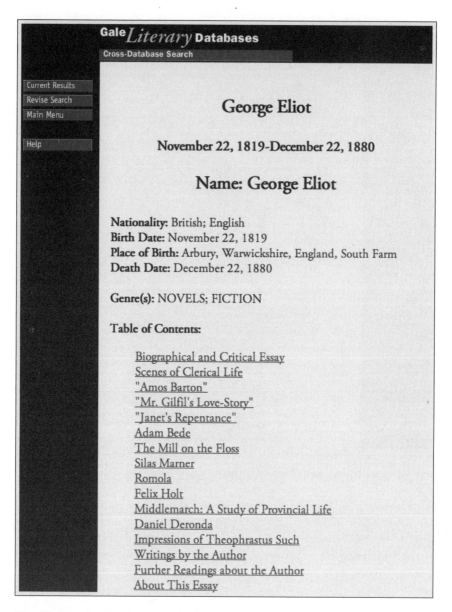

Fig. 37. Result of author search for "George Eliot" as novelist in *Dictionary of Literary Biography.*

you can save a lot of time and improve the quality of your search by taking a few minutes to consult Search Tips in the left margin of the screen.

The Oxford Dictionary of National Biography (ODNB), which is an online biographical database that evolved from the highly regarded, multivolume *Dictionary of National Biography,* could also be consulted for major British authors. The scope of this database is much broader than the *DLB* since it covers important men and women from the British Isles from the fourth century BC to the year 2002. The length of each biographical account is proportionate to the importance of the subject. Shakespeare is accorded forty-nine pages, Keats only fifteen. The *ODNB* is available both online and in print.

There was controversy and discussion among scholars about the accuracy of some of the information, authorship of entries, and similar issues in the *ODNB* at the time of publication. Yet the *ODNB* was also recognized as the best reference source of the year by a number of professional organizations. This kind of intellectual difference of opinion is not unusual among scholars. Even the most authoritative and highly regarded sources sometimes have errors, and scholars sometimes disagree with one another. So it never hurts to check your information in a second source. The online version of *ODNB* has one major advantage over its printed counterpart: errors can be corrected as found, and revisions and updates can be included on a regular basis. In the *ODNB,* these changes are made three times a year.

The equivalent of the *ODNB* on this side of the Atlantic is the *American National Biography (ANB),* available both as a database and as a multivolume reference set. Although primarily an expanded version of the classic *Dictionary of American Biography (DAB),* the *ANB* includes many influential people of various ethnic and racial minority groups who are not found in the *DAB.* Critics have also lamented that many distinguished American women are absent from the original *DAB.* Although the new *American National Biography* has much better coverage of women, you may also find it useful to consult *Notable American Women* for deceased American women writers, which is available only in print.

There are likely to be many other single-volume biographical dictionaries of literary figures in your library's reference collection. These afford each author only a factual paragraph or two, but for basic data they may be perfectly adequate. Several are mentioned in the appendix.

Don't forget that you can find citations for biographies of individual authors in the online catalog. Most general encyclopedias, like *Britannica Online* or the printed *Encyclopædia Britannica*, have biographical information.

In Quest of Quotations

In writing your term papers, you will undoubtedly use quotations from your primary sources as documentation for your thesis. Most likely you will have noted the important passages in your copy of the novel, poem, play, or short story. But once in a while you will need to track down an elusive quotation to substantiate a point you wish to make. With so many primary texts becoming more and more available in electronic format, it has become increasingly easy to search the databases of these works by keyword or by a partially remembered phrase. Two such databases are *Black Drama, 1850–Present* and *Victorian Women Writers Online*. As we indicated in chapter 1, many libraries will supply a handy list of their electronic text databases by discipline. Such a list is often the easiest way to identify these databases. If these sources are not available, there are a couple of printed reference sources to assist you.

The printed concordance is an alphabetical index to all substantial words in an individual work or in a body of works. Concordances exist to different versions of the Bible and to the works of many major authors, such as Shakespeare. It is easy to appreciate the usefulness of this type of reference tool. If you were looking for the line in Hamlet "there is special providence in the fall of the sparrow," you could waste considerable time and energy thumbing randomly through your copy of the play, or you could consult *The Harvard Concordance to Shakespeare*. To track down the quotation in the concordance, simply check the choices under one of the three keywords in the line: *fall, providence,* and *sparrow. The Harvard Concordance to Shake-*

speare has three columns of choices under *fall*. Under *providence*, however, there are only six quotations, the sixth being the one you want (fig. 38). It is in *Hamlet*, act 5, scene 2, line 220. The "P" following the citations indicates a prose passage as opposed to one in verse. If your library has a concordance to the works of a specific author, the formal subject headings in the online catalog is under the formal subject heading of the author's name and the subdivision "Concordance," as in "Shakespeare, William, 1564–1616—Concordance." You could also find this concordance by doing a keyword search in your online catalog, linking the words "Shakespeare" and "concordance" with "and."

You are not going to find a concordance for every author. And the works of some authors may not be included in any of the full-text literary databases offering keyword searching. If the quotation is fairly well known, it may appear in a dictionary of general quotations such as *The Oxford Dictionary of Quotations* or Bartlett's *Familiar Quotations*, which is also online. All these dictionaries, some of which are mentioned in the appendix, are selective, but all include some important quotations from literature. And, as you can see in the next section, one special English-language dictionary, the *Oxford English*

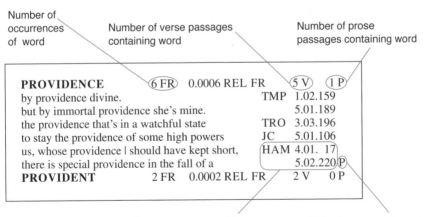

Fig. 38. Finding a line from *Hamlet* in *The Harvard Concordance to Shakespeare* (1002). The listings identify passages by type (prose and verse) and location.

Dictionary, can also serve as a dictionary of quotations in its electronic version.

Facts from Dictionaries and Handbooks

When you need quick information, such as a definition of a word or the history of a literary concept, you head for an English-language dictionary or a literary handbook. You may already own an abridged English-language dictionary or have access to one online. Good, inexpensive versions in electronic format or hard- or softcover have been available from Merriam-Webster, Random House, and Funk and Wagnalls for years. They will usually suffice for everyday problems of spelling, pronunciation, and definition. In addition, the spell-check features of most word-processing software can assist with spelling. When these fail to solve your problem, an unabridged dictionary, like *Webster's Third New International Dictionary of the English Language*, should be your next recourse. Whereas abridged dictionaries are limited to the most frequently used words, the unabridged strive to contain all known words in the language with the possible exception of some slang or colloquial terms. Your college library most likely has an ample supply of both abridged and unabridged dictionaries. Most also provide access to some online dictionaries, such as *Cambridge Dictionaries Online*, which includes the *International Dictionary of English*, *Dictionary of American English*, *International Dictionary of Phrasal Verbs*, *International Dictionary of Idioms*, and *Learner's Dictionary*.

As you study literature from earlier centuries, an etymological dictionary will prove invaluable. For every word ever known to exist in a particular language, this kind of dictionary supplies a history, the date of the word's first known recorded use, variant spellings and pronunciations, and distinctive usages. The *Oxford English Dictionary (OED)* is an excellent example, available both online and in print. If you wanted to examine the possible meanings of the term *nunnery* in Hamlet's famous command to Ophelia, "Get thee to a nunnery!" (*Ham.* 3.1.121), you would have to consult the *OED*. According to the *OED* online, the term can mean either "a residence for a community of nuns" or "a brothel." Since the sec-

1. a. A place of residence for a community of nuns; a building or group of buildings in which nuns live as a religious community; a convent. Also *fig.*

. . .

b. *slang.* A brothel. Now *hist.*

. . .

1593 T. NASHE *Christs Teares* 79b, [To] some one Gentleman generally acquainted, they giue..free priuiledge thenceforward in theyr Nunnery, to procure them frequentance. **1594** *Gesta Grayorum* (1914) 12 Lucy Negro, Abbess de Clerkenwell, holdeth the Nunnery of Clerkenwell. *a*1625 J. FLETCHER *Mad Lover* IV. ii, in F. Beaumont & J. Fletcher *Comedies & Trag.* (1647) sig. C4ᵛ/1, *Chi.* Ther's an old Nunnerie at hand. *Clo.* What's that. *Chi.* A bawdie House. **1781** *Compl. Mod. London Spy* (title-page), The characters of many well-known Persons who are now frequenters at Gaming-Houses, Bagnios, and other Nunneries, Night-Houses,..Taverns, [etc.]. **1785** F. GROSE *Classical Dict. Vulgar Tongue, Nunnery*, a bawdy house. **1846** *Swell's Night Guide* 126/2 *Nunnery*, a brothel. **1977** J. T. SHIPLEY *In Praise of Eng.* 194 To the antipapist Tudors *nunnery* was a slang term for a *brothel.*

Fig. 39. Portions of the definition of *nunnery* from the *Oxford English Dictionary Online.*

ond usage was apparently introduced by Thomas Nashe in 1593, it would have been known during Shakespeare's time (fig. 39). Unlike the printed version of the *OED*, which limits you to looking up a specific word, the electronic version offers more search paths through its advanced-search options at the bottom of the screen. Among other uses, this advanced-search feature makes it possible to search the quotation from Nashe's poem that was included in the definition for *nunnery*. With the advanced features, you can search by word or combination of words, making it possible to find quotations as long as the quotation you need is among the examples provided in the dictionary.

For general information on an author or literary period, for the identification of characters, or for definitions of literary terms, a handbook is your best tool. *The Oxford Encyclopedia of American Literature, The Oxford Companion to English Literature,* and *The Oxford Companion to Women's Writing in the United States* are excellent, easy-to-use, single-volume handbooks. Each has basic biographical information about authors, brief plot summaries of major works, short definitions of literary terms and concepts, and general outlines of literary movements. For example, if you need some background information on the epistolary novel in the context of American women authors, *The Oxford Companion to Women's Writings in the United States* offers an excellent brief essay (fig. 40). Each of these three handbooks focuses on a nationality or gender; others, like the *New Princeton Encyclopedia of Poetry and Poetics*, are organized around specific genres. It is a good idea to consult a handbook whenever you do not clearly understand some term. Several other literary handbooks and English-language dictionaries are noted in the appendix.

EPISTOLARY NOVEL. Although American women have produced few epistolary novels, the literary significance of those that exist is much greater than simple numbers would suggest. Since an epistolary novel is composed of an exchange of *letters, a correspondence among its characters, it does not contain the explicit guiding, framing, and potentially dominating presence of a narrative persona. The epistolary novel offers readers direct and potentially equal access to the voices of its characters. For this reason, the epistolary novel has served as a vehicle for authors who wish to present voices marginal to the dominant cultural experience—voices traditionally muted or submerged. From Hannah Webster *Foster's *The Coquette* (1797), to Alice *Walker's *The Color Purple* (1982), Ana *Castillo's *The Mixquiahuala Letters* (1986), and Lee *Smith's *Fair and Tender Ladies* (1988), the epistolary novel has offered women writers a way to privilege voices that might not otherwise be heard.

The epistolary novel emerged in eighteenth-century Europe from the tradition of genteel

Fig. 40. A portion of the entry "epistolary novel" in *The Oxford Companion to Women's Writings in the United States* (275).

CHAPTER EIGHT

One-Stop Shopping

As noted in earlier chapters, there is a growing trend toward linking together the different kinds of information found in electronic databases, making it easier for researchers to locate all or most of the information they need. For example, you may want factual, biographical information on an author; a list of the author's works along with a copy of some of them; and a list of critical books and articles pertaining to one or more of these literary works. To acquire all this information, you normally would need to check each database or printed reference work separately. Increasingly, the database producers are providing links among their many electronic products and other databases. Two such sources are *Literature Online (LION)* and *Literature Resource Center*, which we discussed in chapter 3.

LION is a conglomerate of separate literary collections currently offered on microfilm or electronically by the publisher Chadwick-Healey. It includes links to other sources not published by Chadwick-Healey, like the *Annual Bibliography of English Language and Literature (ABELL)*, *JSTOR* (the full text of some major scholarly journals) and the *MLA International Bibliography*. (Your library must also subscribe to *JSTOR* and the *MLA International Bibliography* for those links in *LION* to be activated.) By pulling all these reference sources together, *LION* allows you to find biographical information on English and American authors, lists of their works, the text of many of these primary sources, lists of secondary critical studies

pertaining to these works, audio readings of the author's works, and
relevant Web sites. In some cases, you can go directly to the online
full text of the articles or works cited. Note that an edition of a poem
or novel provided in *LION* may not be the most authoritative or one
that your instructor wants you to use for your class; it may simply be
an edition that is not protected by copyright. So it is always wise to
consult first with your instructor about editions to use.

   Literature Resource Center covers much of the same information as
LION but contains no primary texts. Since you are already familiar
with *Literature Resource Center* from chapter 3, let's look at a typical
search using *LION*. The initial screen tells you a bit about the scope of
this tool: more than 350,000 works of literature, one hundred and fifty
journals in full text, and other literary criticism. The database cross-
searches the *MLA International Bibliography* and the *Annual Bibliography of English Language and Literature (ABELL)*; it has Open
URL linking and other features. If you want to search the entire database, simply type the name of the author or literary work in the Quick
Search box in the upper left corner of the main screen (fig. 41). Let's

Fig. 41. Home page for *Literature Online*.

assume you want information on the author Thomas Hardy. A quick
search of the database yields an initial summary panel of results:
1 general biographical entry on Hardy, 922 texts of his poetry, 11 texts
of his prose works, 8,005 works of criticism, 6 Web sites, 7 readings of
his poetry in multimedia, and a few other kinds of materials (fig. 42).
Notice the icons in the box labeled Key. These will be found adjacent
to each entry and will indicate if there is full text or a page image
of the actual text of the article or whether it is just the bibliographic
record. Also, you will know whether the citation was taken from the
MLA International Bibliography or *ABELL* or whether the full text of
an article came from *JSTOR*. You can scroll through the list of items

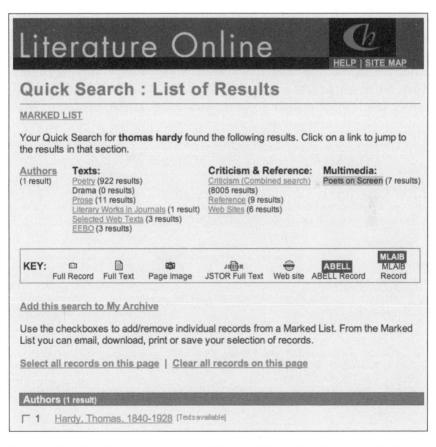

Fig. 42. Results of author search for "Thomas Hardy" in *Literature Online*.

matching your search and place an "x" in the box next to any of the
entries you wish to keep as you sort through for items that look most
promising. You can also click directly on any entry you wish to see at
this time. Unless you are doing very comprehensive research on this
author or unless your author is much less prolific than Hardy, you will
probably want to narrow the scope of your search rather than browse
through thousands of items by or about the author.

To narrow the search, let's return for a moment to that first
screen (fig. 41). If you know that you need specific kinds of information, you can limit your search to the options listed below the
Quick Search screen: Authors, Texts, and Criticism and Reference.
Perhaps you are really looking for literary criticism of Hardy's novel
Tess of the d'Urbervilles. If you choose Criticism and Reference and
type the title of this novel in the space for Keywords (fig. 43), you
will find that you have pared down your results considerably, from
8,005 works of criticism to 573 that pertain directly to this novel.
(In some of the first hits, the author of the article may be named
Tess, for example.) As you peruse the list, notice that some citations
were culled from the *MLA International Bibliography* and some from

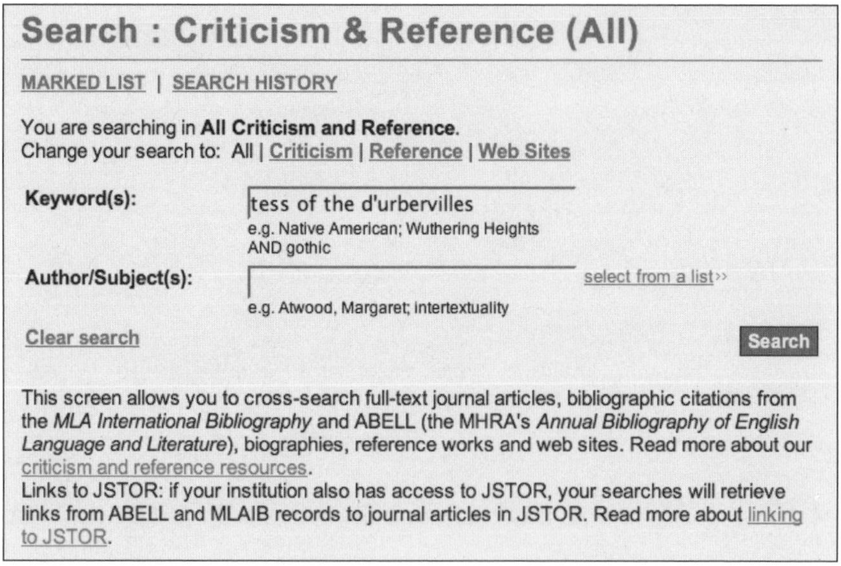

Fig. 43. Search for literary criticism on *Tess of the d'Urbervilles* in
Literature Online.

ABELL (fig. 44). On occasion you can link directly to the full text of the article. Unfortunately, there does not appear to be any effort to eliminate duplicate listings from these two bibliographies (fig. 45).

As with many public online catalogs or other databases, you can save the results from your searches to My Archive for later use. This step can save you a lot of time if you plan to do your research in stages and don't want to have to repeat searches each time you return to your research.

LION offers several other ways to browse its databases. Returning to the initial screen, you can peruse the contents of the books indexed, search a list of the full-text journals it covers, scan the author index, or search through the list of poets on screen (fig. 41). These browsing indexes will usually not be that helpful, but on a few occasions they can be. If your search by author, text, or criticism and reference has not been especially productive, browsing the author index or scanning some of the contents or the titles of books indexed might help you devise a more effective search strategy. These browsing indexes can also give you an idea of which sources are indexed in *LION* and which are not. There is no single database that will search all the online sources in literature. It always helps, as you are becoming familiar with a database, to examine the tools that are included.

You can also consult Information Centre for a description of *LION*'s coverage and instructions on how to use this database most effectively. There is even an online demonstration. At any time during your searches, you can click on Help at the top of the screen for instructions and searching tips. Do not hesitate to consult the Help screens as you

---

☐ 24 ▫ 📄 📷	**ABELL** Lovesey, Oliver.: "Reconstructing Tess." Studies in English Literature 1500-1900 (43:4) 2003, 913-38. (2003)
☐ 25 ▫ 📄 📷	**MLAIB** Lovesey, Oliver: "Reconstructing Tess" SEL: Studies in English Literature, 1500-1900, (43:4), 2003 Autumn, 913-38. (2003)
☐ 26 ▫ 📄	**ABELL** Moran, Maureen.: review of Murphy, Patricia. "Time is of the essence: temporality, gender, and the New Woman." English Literature in Transition (46:2) 2003, 181-4. (2003)

Fig. 44. Some results of keyword search for literary criticism on *Tess of the d'Urbervilles* in *Literature Online*.

Criticism & Reference : List of Results (Criticism)

MARKED LIST | SEARCH HISTORY | MODIFY SEARCH | NEW SEARCH

You searched for:
Keyword(s): tess of the d'urbervilles

Literature Online found the following results:

▶ Criticism : Criticism search [587 entries, 827 hits]	Reference » [21 entries, 45 hits]	Web Sites » [7 entries, 13 hits]

Add this search to My Archive

Use the checkboxes to add/remove individual records from a Marked List. From the Marked List you can email, download, print or save your selection of records.

Select all records on this page | Clear all records on this page

KEY:	🖾 Full Record	🖹 Full Text	📷 Page Image	JSTOR JSTOR Full Text	ABELL ABELL Record	MLAIB MLAIB Record

Page(s): **1** | 2 | 3 | 4 | 5 | 6 | 7 | 8 | 9 | 10 | Next>>

☐ 1 🖾 MLAIB Efron, Arthur; Irwin, Michael (foreword): "Experiencing Tess of the D'Urbervilles: A Deweyan Account" Amsterdam, Netherlands: Rodopi, 2005. xiii, 248 pp.. (Value Inquiry Book Series 162). (2005)
🔗 InfoLink

☐ 2 🖾 ABELL Clarke, John Stock; Law, Graham.: "More light on the serial publication of *Tess of the d'Urbervilles*." Thomas Hardy Journal (20:2) 2004, 49-56. (2004)
🔗 InfoLink

☐ 3 🖾 MLAIB Clarke, John Stock; Law, Graham: "More Light on the Serial Publication of Tess of the D'Urbervilles" Thomas Hardy Journal, (20:2), 2004 June, 49-56. (2004)
🔗 InfoLink

Fig. 45. Duplicate listings, from the *MLA International Bibliography* and from *ABELL*, in results of a keyword search in *Literature Online*.

get acquainted with this database or if you are having difficulty conducting a search.

Like most reference databases, *LION* is routinely updated with new sources and enhanced searching options. Occasionally consult the What's New? selection on the opening screen, even if you become an experienced searcher of this database, to learn what changes have been made since you last used it.

Both *LION* and *Literature Resource Center* represent the kind of one-stop shopping for literary information that most users are seeking in their electronic reference sources. Undoubtedly there will be others in the future.

There is also software available in some libraries that will allow the user to search, with a single command, a group of databases, specified by the user. In other words, it is possible in some libraries for people to create their own consolidated tool of databases that are most pertinent to their interests in English and American literature and search them all at one time rather than one by one. Your librarian can best advise you on whether your library has this capability for "federated searching" and whatever features and limitations your library's software may have. The librarian can also offer suggestions on how to use this service most effectively.

CHAPTER NINE

Managing Citations

As you prepare the final draft of your term paper, you will undoubtedly want to make sure that your work, especially its documentation and bibliography, is presented in an acceptable form. The *MLA Handbook for Writers of Research Papers* describes the conventions for written literary research that are approved by scholars and college professors. It briefly discusses the process of selecting and researching a topic as well as the mechanics of writing critical prose. There are over a hundred examples of reference notes and bibliographic entries intended to illustrate the citation of every conceivable kind of source that you might use, including those in electronic format. Sample pages of a research paper are given, too, to help you set up your paper according to the recommended format. A detailed index makes this handbook particularly easy to use. The most recent edition of the *MLA Handbook*, the sixth, is most likely available at your library, but if you plan to write many literary research papers, you will want to obtain your own copy.

There are several other popular style manuals that will also work for most sources cited in literary research papers. *The Chicago Manual of Style* and *Publication Manual of the American Psychological Association* both contain chapters on research and writing and will likely serve your needs as well. The *Chicago Manual* began initially as a simple style sheet for those who wished to publish with the University of Chicago Press, but it evolved into a book-length manual that includes, among other features, examples of citations for a variety of publications in all formats. Similarly, the examples and text in the APA's *Publications Manual*, while most useful for those in psychology, may be perfectly appropriate for your work. Some professors may have a preference about how you cite your sources in your paper, so it is always worth checking with the professor if no preference is indicated in your course syllabus.

Those of you who are especially computer-literate will be pleased to know there is software that helps you manage your bibliographic citations. These products will automatically convert the bibliographic information for articles that you download from electronic databases, such as the *MLA International Bibliography*, into the proper citation format according to the *MLA Handbook* or other style manuals. Three—*Reference Manager, EndNote,* and *ProCite*—have been around for a while but are sold as individual subscriptions, making it difficult for many libraries to offer the software widely on all their public computers. (*Reference Manager* can be networked among a number of computers on a small local area network). But for those students who write a lot of papers, are managing many bibliographic citations, or plan to go to graduate school, a personal subscription to one of these software products makes sense. A newer product called *RefWorks* is Web-based and can be acquired as an individual subscription or through a campus-wide license. The license makes the software accessible to everyone at your college or university. The features offered by these products vary, and, as with most software, new versions with new enhancements are issued regularly. Your needs will determine which features are preferable.

Ask your librarian if your campus has specific software for managing citations. Many libraries offer instructional seminars in the use of the citation-managing software that is available in the libraries or most commonly used on campus. For more information on these tools, see the appendix.

CHAPTER TEN

Guides to Research in Literature

Throughout this guide we have concentrated on literary research, emphasizing only about thirty reference sources. Of course, many other indexes, bibliographies, dictionaries, handbooks, databases and related tools may become helpful as you develop your knowledge and skills in the study of English and American literature. These works are cited in literary guides that provide broader coverage than is appropriate here.

The most extensive current guide to research tools in British, American, and other English-language literatures is James L. Harner's *Literary Research Guide*. Annotations are provided for most entries, accurately describing the reference sources and evaluating their overall quality and usefulness. If you have extensive research projects or plan to continue your literary studies in graduate school, you should, or rather must, become familiar with this excellent guide.

No discussion of research guides would be complete without some mention of Robert Balay's *Guide to Reference Books*. Listing all major reference books in all disciplines, this is the reference librarian's right hand. It is without a doubt the most comprehensive bibliography of reference sources currently available. Most entries are annotated.

Its organization, first by discipline and then by type of reference tool, makes it especially easy to use. Previous editions of this book were written by Eugene Sheehy, and many experienced librarians may still refer to it as Sheehy.

These two guides to literature, along with two others, are listed in the appendix.

Selective Bibliography of Reference Sources for English and American Literature

American National Biography. New York: Oxford UP, 1999. Print. 2000– . Online.
ANB replaces the classic *Dictionary of American Biography*, presenting the lives of more than 17,500 men and women from diverse backgrounds and all periods of American history. The online version is updated quarterly, with new entries and revisions of entries to enhance accuracy and currency. There are now over 18,300 entries in the online version, a thousand more than in the original printed version. The online version is searchable by keywords and phrases, subject name, gender, occupation, birth date, birthplace, death date, and contributor name. The print index is arranged by name of subject, name of contributor, place of birth in the United States (by state), occupation, and "realm of renown."

American Periodical Series Online, 1740–1900. Ann Arbor: ProQuest Information and Learning.
This collection contains digitized images of the pages of American magazines and journals that originated between 1741 and 1900. *APS Online* features over 1,100 periodicals spanning nearly two hundred

years—from colonial times to the advent of American involvement in World War II.

Andrews, William L., Francis Smith Foster, and Trudier Harris. *The Oxford Companion to African American Literature*. New York: Oxford UP, 1997.
This handbook, specifically devoted to African American literature, features biographical profiles; descriptions of important works; literary characters, genres, and customs. The companion often contains biographical information on authors not easily found in other reference books.

Annual Bibliography of English Language and Literature. Cambridge: Mod. Humanities Research Assn., 1921– . Online and print.
This bibliography of English and American literature indexes books, pamphlets, dissertations, and periodical articles. References to book reviews are placed alongside citations for books. The language section is arranged by subject, the literature section by literary period. The index for literary authors, subjects, and critical authors makes this bibliography particularly easy to use. Entries from this bibliography also appear in *Literature Online (LION)*.

Balay, Robert, ed. *Guide to Reference Books*. 11th ed. Chicago: Amer. Lib. Assn., 1996.
This guide provides the broadest coverage of major scholarly research tools in all disciplines through 1993. Brief annotations accompany most entries. The literature section is subdivided by type of reference source, by languages or nationality, and by author. The index interfiles authors, editors, titles, and subject entries.

Bartlett, John. *Familiar Quotations*. 17th ed. Boston: Little, 2002.
This standard collection of quotations has a keyword index that directs the reader to their authors. Selections listed under the same author are arranged chronologically. The tenth edition is available over the Internet from Columbia University's *Project Bartleby* (www.bartleby.com/100).

Book Review Digest. New York: Wilson, 1905– . Print and online.
The oldest book review index, this standard resource is available online and continues to be published in print format. *Book Review Digest Plus* lists book review references from over eight thousand periodicals from 1983 to the present; many of the reviews are available in full text. Also available is the *Book Review Digest Retrospective, 1905–1982*.

Book Review Index. Detroit: Gale, 1965–69; 1972– . Print and online.
More than six hundred publications are indexed: journals, general periodicals, and newspapers. *Book Review Index Online* is an index to book reviews that has more than five million citations from thousands

of publications. *Book Review Index Online Plus* lists more than 634,000 full-text reviews from *InfoTrac OneFile* and *InfoTrac Expanded Academic* and offers accessibility to full text through links to what the library owns.

Bordman, Gerald, ed. *The Oxford Companion to American Theatre.* 3rd ed. New York: Oxford UP, 2004.

Although his handbook concentrates on American stage productions as opposed to written drama, students of literature can find a considerable amount of information here, especially in the entries for several hundred major American plays.

Bracken, James K. *Reference Works in British and American Literature.* 2 vols. 2nd ed. Englewood: Libs. Unlimited, 1998.

Volume 1 covers reference works, major journals, research centers, and associations in English and American literature. The arrangement is classified, and there are author-title and subject indexes. The annotations are lengthy and often evaluative. Volume 2 covers individual authors.

The Chicago Manual of Style. 15th ed. Chicago: U of Chicago P, 2003. CD-ROM version, 2004.

This comprehensive manual for authors, editors, proofreaders, indexers, and others involved in publishing evolved from a single sheet of typographic fundamentals intended as a guide for the university community of the late nineteenth century. The fifteenth edition has reorganized and updated chapters on documentation, including guidance on citing electronic sources.

CIS U.S. Congressional Committee Hearings Index, 1833–1969. Washington: Congressional Information Service, 1981–85.

This printed index to congressional hearings covers the period from 1833 to 1969. The electronic version is *Lexis Nexis Congressional Historical Indexes*, an online source that includes the *Congressional Indexes*, 1789–1969, and *Indexes to Unpublished Hearings* through 1980.

Combined Retrospective Index to Book Reviews in Humanities Journals, 1802–1974. Woodbridge: Research Publications, 1982–84.

This print index is an excellent resource for tracking down reviews of older books. Provides "author and title access to about 500,000 book reviews that appeared in the complete backfiles of over 150 humanities journals" from 1802 to 1974 (1: vii).

Concise Rules of the APA. Washington: Amer. Psychological Assn., 2005.

Although the rules are consistent with the conventions of the *Publications Manual of the American Psychological Association,* the primary audience for this publication is students who are writing papers in social and behavior sciences, not those publishing psychological research.

Contemporary Authors. Farmington Hills. 1962– .
This database covers comprehensive information on 116,000 modern authors. The information is also derived from a printed set of reference books by the same name.

Contemporary Literary Criticism. Detroit: Gale, 1973– . Online (*Literature Resource Center*) and print.
This large, ongoing publication excerpts critiques, published primarily within the last thirty years, of literary works by writers who are living or who have died since 1 January 1960. The content of this set is included in the *Literature Resource Center.* Gale publishes a number of other sources that excerpt literary criticism, including *Black Literature Criticism, Short Story Criticism, Classical and Medieval Literature Criticism, Nineteenth Century Literature Criticism, Poetry Criticism, Literature Criticism from 1400 to 1800,* and *Twentieth Century Literary Criticism.*

Contemporary Novelists. 7th ed. Farmington Hills: Saint James, 2001. E-book ed., 2003.
This volume provides biographies, bibliographies, and critical essays on 650 contemporary writers (a hundred of them new to this edition). This title is now available in e-book form—from a database through *Gale Virtual Reference Library.*

Contemporary Poets. 7th ed. Farmington Hills: Saint James, 2001. E-book ed., 2003.
This tool provides biographies, bibliographies, and critical essays on 787 English language poets, 120 new to this edition. This title is now available in e-book form—from a database through *Gale Virtual Reference Library.*

Davidson, Cathy N., and Linda Wagner-Martin. *The Oxford Companion to Women's Writings in the United States.* New York: Oxford UP, 1995.
This source has a specific focus on the writings of American women and includes some excellent essays on many topics not easily found in similar reference books.

Dictionary of American Biography. 21 vols. New York: Scribner's, 1928– 37. Ten supps., 1844–95.
The *DAB* contains lengthy biographical accounts of prominent deceased Americans. The articles are written and signed by the au-

thoritative contributors. There are six general indexes covering all volumes through the eighth supplement: names of the subjects, contributors of the biographies, birthplaces, schools, occupations, and general topics. The ninth supplement has a name index covering all the supplements.

Drabble, Margaret, ed. *The Oxford Companion to English Literature.* 6th ed. New York: Oxford UP, 2000.
This guide provides short summaries of British literary works, definitions of terms, discussions of movements and trends, and brief biographies and bibliographies of writers.

Early American Imprints: Series I: Evans, 1639–1800. Naples: Readex. Online.
Based on the renowned *American Bibliography,* by Charles Evans. Contains publications for every aspect of life in seventeenth- and eighteenth-century America, from agriculture and auctions through foreign affairs, diplomacy, literature, music, religion, the Revolutionary War, temperance, witchcraft.

Early English Books Online (EEBO). Ann Arbor: Chadwyck-Healy.
Contains digital facsimile page images of virtually every work printed in England, Ireland, Scotland, Wales, and British North America and of works in English printed elsewhere, 1473–1700.

EBSCO Academic Search Premier. Ipswich: EBSCO Information Services. Online.
The database contains indexing for over eight thousand publications, with full text for more than 4,650, in all disciplines.

EndNote 8, Stamford: Thomson ISI ResearchSoft, 2004. *ProCite* 5, Stamford: Thomson ISI ResearchSoft, 2004. *Reference Manager* 11, Stamford: Thomson ISI ResearchSoft, 2004.
All three software tools locate bibliographic data and create bibliographies automatically for term papers in accordance with a wide range of style requirements, including those of the *MLA Handbook. EndNote* and *ProCite* can be used on both a Windows and Mac desktop; *Reference Manager* will only work on Windows. *EndNote* is probably the most popular, although many of the same features are beginning to show up in all three with each new version. All three are limited to the desktop, although *Reference Manager* can be networked in a local area network to share citations, a feature that can be useful in a joint research project.

Expanded Academic ASAP. Farmington Hills: Gale, 1984– . Online.
This online index, described in chapter 3, provides citations and some

full text to articles and book reviews published in several thousand general interest and scholarly periodicals in the humanities, social sciences, and sciences.

FIAF International Filmarchive Database. Silverplatter. Online.
This resource is only online and contains the *International Index to Film Periodicals* (1973–), *International Index to Television Periodicals* (1972–), *Treasures from the Film Archives,* and several other resources. It is particularly good for international films.

Film Literature Index. Albany: Filmdex, 1973– . Print. Indiana U, 1976–2001. Online.
Available in print from 1973 and online for the years 1976–2001, this source lists citations to film, television and video articles, reviews and book reviews.

Film Review Index. Phoenix: Oryx, 1986–1987. Print.
This two-volume retrospective bibliography lists articles and books on selected films and provides citations to reviews, histories, and critical commentary for over seven thousand films, covering the years 1882 to 1985.

Gibaldi, Joseph. *MLA Handbook for Writers of Research Papers.* 6th ed. New York: MLA, 2003.
This handbook presents rules for documenting quotations, facts, opinion, and information that is paraphrased in research papers. There are lots of tips for writing a good research paper. The sixth edition provides more guidelines than the fifth did for doing research on the Internet and for evaluating the reliability of sites. There is also a chapter on what constitutes plagiarism and how to avoid it.

Grassian, Esther. *Thinking Critically about World Wide Web Resources.* June 1995. 1995– <http://www.library.ucla.edu/libraries/college/help/critical/index.htm>. *Thinking Critically about Discipline-Based World Wide Web Resources.* 10 Oct. 1997. 1997– <http://www.library.ucla.edu/libraries/college/help/critical/discipline.htm>. UCLA College Lib. Regents of the U of California.
Written by a veteran librarian at UCLA's College Library, these concise lists identify a number of factors to consider when looking at Web sites.

Harner, James L. *Literary Research Guide: An Annotated Listing of Reference Sources in English Literary Studies.* 4th ed. New York: MLA, 2002.
This standard guide provides an extensive list of important reference books and periodicals on British and American literature and other literatures in English. The annotations are evaluative, offering keen ob-

servations on the quality and usefulness of specific reference sources. In his preface to the fourth edition, Harner claims to have "assessed anew each of the works cited in the third edition and evaluated reference works, print and electronic, that appeared after April 1997" (ix).

Hart, James D., ed. *The Oxford Companion to American Literature.* 6th ed. New York: Oxford UP, 1995.
Like its counterpart for English literature, this source provides short summaries of American literary works, definitions of terms, discussions of movements and trends, and brief biographies and bibliographies of writers.

Humanities Index. New York: Wilson, 1975–. Online and print.
This index has a long history. Entitled *International Index to Periodicals* from 1920 to 1955 and *Social Sciences and Humanities Index* from 1965 to 1974, it furnishes easy access to articles in nearly three hundred periodicals for the humanities. The print version features author and subject indexing, making it an especially good source for interdisciplinary topics. A compilation of book reviews concludes each issue. Several vendors offer this index as an online database, titled *Humanities Abstracts.*

Index to Book Reviews in the Humanities. Williamston: Thomson, 1960– 90. Print.
This annual index lists book reviews of secondary sources in the humanities from over seven hundred scholarly periodicals from 1960 to 1990. It is particularly useful for tracking down scholars' responses to new literary criticism, but it provides no excerpts from the reviews.

Joseph, Nancy L. *Research Writing Using Traditional and Electronic Sources.* Upper Saddle River: Prentice, 1999.
This practical and readable book guides students through the entire research process. The sections on evaluating print and online sources are excellent and illustrated with examples. A study companion for the book is available on the Web at http://cwx.prenhall .com/bookbind/pubbooks/joseph/.

JSTOR. 2005 <http://www.jstor.org>.
JSTOR offers noncurrent issues of major scholarly journals in many disciplines. If your library subscribes to *JSTOR*, you can search the database for articles by subject. Some of the literature journals are *African American Review, American Literature, ELH,* and *Shakespeare Quarterly.*

Lexis Nexis Congressional Historical Indexes. See *CIS U.S. Congressional Committee Hearings Index.*

Library of Congress Subject Headings. 27th ed. Washington: Lib. of Congress. 2004.
These volumes list the terms and phrases used as formal subject headings in online catalogs.

Literary Resources on the Net. 2005 <http://andromeda.rutgers.edu/~jlynch/>.
Created and maintained by Jack Lynch, associate professor of English at the Newark campus of Rutgers University, this page lists Web sites devoted to English and American literature.

Literature Online. Alexandria: Chadwick-Healey, 1996– . Online.
This database represents the largest collection of literary texts and includes primary sources (poems, plays, and novels) and secondary sources (reference works and citations to literary criticism). *LION* can offer the user one-stop shopping for background on an author, copies of works, and an index to major literary criticism (some with the full text linked to the citation).

Literature Resource Center. Farmington Hills: Gale, 1998– . Online.
This database conveniently includes biographical information, bibliographic listings of author's works, and critical analyses of more than 122,000 authors. Unlike *Literature Online*, it does not include primary texts.

Mainiero, Lina, ed. *American Women Writers: A Critical Reference Guide from Colonial Times to the Present*. 4 vols. New York: Ungar, 1979–82. Supp., 1994.
This source provides biographical information and critical discussions on well-known and little-known American women writers of fiction and nonfiction, encompassing three centuries. A two-volume abridged edition was published in 1982.

Making of America. Cornell U Lib. 2005 <http://cdl.library.cornell.edu/moa/>.
Making of America is a major collaborative endeavor of Cornell University and the University of Michigan to preserve and make accessible through digital technology a significant body of primary sources related to development of the United States.

Merriam-Webster Online. Springfield: Merriam, 2002– .
This dictionary is really several databases, including the *Encyclopædia Britannica*, *Merriam-Webster Online* (dictionary and thesaurus), *Merriam-Webster Unabridged* (dictionary), *Merriam-Webster Collegiate* (dictionary), and *Merriam-Webster for Kids*. An individual library may

subscribe to all or some of these databases. There are also printed versions of these sources available.

MLA International Bibliography of Books and Articles on the Modern Languages and Literatures. New York: MLA, 1922– . Online and print.
From 1922 through 1955, this source listed only studies written by Americans. In 1956, it began international coverage by including writers from other countries. Since 1969, the scope has been further expanded to include books, dissertations, essays in Festschriften, and articles in over two thousand international periodicals. As of spring 2006, the electronic versions list articles published since 1926.

MRQE–Movie Review Query Engine. Stewart M. Clamen, 1993–2005. Online.
This Internet movie review index provide links to over 120,000 full-text reviews covering more than 17,000 films from international, national, and local newspapers, arts and entertainment journals, and other sources.

New Princeton Encyclopedia of Poetry and Poetics. Princeton UP, 1993.
According to the introductory material, "this is a book of knowledge, of facts, theories, questions, and informed judgment, about poetry. Its aim is to provide a comprehensive, comparative, reasonably advanced, yet readable reference for all students, teachers, scholars, poets, or general readers interested in the history of any poetry in any national literatures of the world, or in any aspect of the technique or criticism of poetry" (vii).

New York Theatre Critics' Reviews, New York: Critics' Theatre Reviews, Inc., 1995. Print.
This is a review source for Broadway and some Off-Broadway shows running from 1950 to 1994. Reviews are reprinted in full from various sources such as *The New York Times, New York Post, Time* and other publications. There are cumulative indexes for 1940–1960, 1961–1972, and 1973–1981.

New York Times, 1851–2001. ProQuest Historical Newspapers.
This full-text, electronic version of the newspaper is available through many academic and public libraries.

New York Times Index. New York. 1851– .
The printed subject index to the *New York Times* covers the period from 1851 to the present.

Nineteenth-Century Masterfile. Reston: Paratext, 1999– . Online.
This electronic index of periodicals from the nineteenth century includes references to book reviews. It contains *Poole's Index to Periodical*

Literature as well as several other indexes to periodicals and government publications, from 1802 to the early twentieth century.

Notable American Women, 1607–1950. 3 vols. Cambridge: Harvard UP, 1971. Supp. by *Notable American Women: The Modern Period,* 1980.
Most of the 1,350 biographical accounts in the three main volumes do not duplicate material in the *DAB.*

The Oxford Dictionary of National Biography. New York: Oxford UP, 2004.
This online biographical database evolved from the multivolume *Dictionary of National Biography,* which could also be consulted for major British authors. The scope of this database covers men and women who contributed to British history, from the fourth century BC to 2001. There is also a fifty-volume print edition.

Oxford Dictionary of Quotations. 6th ed. New York: Oxford UP, 2004.
Considered one of the most literary of the quotation dictionaries, the dictionary provides a useful complement to the more general Bartlett's *Familiar Quotations.* Each entry includes details of the earliest traceable source of the quotation, biographical cross-references, birth and death dates, and similar information. Thematic and keyword indexes make it especially easily to find quotations.

Oxford English Dictionary. 2nd ed. 20 vols. Oxford: Clarendon-Oxford UP, 1989.
The *Oxford English Dictionary* is the guide to the meaning, history, and pronunciation of over half a million words, both present and past. It traces the usage of words from across the English-speaking world, through 2.5 million quotations from a wide range of international English language source. It is the best source for etymological analysis and in listing of variant spellings. The second edition of the *OED* is currently available as a twenty-volume print edition (with a three-volume Additions Series), on CD-ROM and also online as the *OED Online.* The online version is updated quarterly with at least a thousand new and revised entries.

Palmer's Index to the Times *Newspaper, 1790–1941.* London: Palmer, 1868–1943.
A printed subject index to the *Times* (London). After 1906, an index was also published by the *Times.*

Parini, Jay, ed. *The Oxford Encyclopedia of American Literature.* New York: Oxford UP, 2004.
This encyclopedia includes 250 essays on poets, playwrights, essayists, and novelists; fifty entries on major works in American literature; as

well as essays on literary movements, periods, and themes. With each entry comes a bibliography of primary and secondary sources and useful cross-references to other pertinent entries.

Parliamentary Debates, 1803–. London. 1804–.
Generally cited as *Hansard* or *Hansard's Parliamentary Debates*, this set indexes the debates of the House of Lords and the House of Commons.

Poole's Index to Periodical Literature, 1802–1881; supplements, 1882–1906. Boston: Houghton, 1802–1906. Print.
This print resource includes references to book reviews. It also forms a part of the *Nineteenth-Century Masterfile* and can thus be searched online. *Poole's* is the major subject index to American and English periodicals published during the nineteenth century. Biographical and critical references to authors are listed under the author's name.

Project MUSE. Johns Hopkins UP. <http://muse.jhu.edu>.
Project MUSE provides online subscription access to the full texts of about three hundred journal titles from sixty scholarly publishers. Literary titles include *Eighteenth Century Studies, Modern Fiction Studies, New Literary History,* and the *Yale Journal of Criticism.*

ProQuest Research Library. ProQuest Research Lib. Ann Arbor: ProQuest Information and Learning, 1971–. Online.
This online index, described in the source list for chapter 3, provides access to over 2,600 journal titles in the humanities, social sciences, and sciences. Many of the journal articles are available in full text. It indexes and often provides full text for reviews from scholarly, general-interest, and newspaper publications. A useful feature is the ability to limit the search to book, film, and theater reviews.

Publication Manual of the American Psychological Association. 5th ed. Washington: Amer. Psychological Assn., 2001.
This manual outlines the conventions of the American Psychological Association for research in social and behavior sciences.

Reader's Guide Retrospective. New York: Wilson, 1997–.
A database containing comprehensive indexing of the most popular general-interest periodicals published in the United States, from 1890 to 1982.

Reader's Guide to Periodical Literature. New York: Wilson, 1905–.
The *Reader's Guide* started publication in 1901 with limited coverage and in 1905 was expanded to include additional periodical titles. All titles are United States publications. Still published today, this index

is particularly valuable for the first seventy-five years of the twentieth century, for which fewer indexing sources are available. *Reader's Guide* is also available electronically.

RefWorks. Bethesda: CSA, 2004. Online.
This is the one bibliographic management software that is Web-based and can be used with any major Web browser on any platform. *RefWorks* can import citations from the standard electronic databases as well as from *EndNote, ProCite,* and *Reference Manager.* Because it is accessible over the Internet, it can be accessed from any Internet-connected computer at any time, and the files can easily be shared by those working jointly on a reference project.

Rodrigues, Dawn. *The Research Paper and the World Wide Web.* 2nd ed. Upper Saddle River: Prentice, 2000.
The author provides detailed information on using the Web for research, covering everything from navigation to using e-mail and newsgroups as research tools. Especially helpful is her chapter "Library and Web Resources," which provides clear examples of what can be found at no cost on the Web and what is proprietary information available only by subscription. Supplemental information can be found on the publisher's Web site at http://cwx.prenhall.com/bookbind/pubbooks/rodrigues.

Spevack, Marvin. *The Harvard Concordance to Shakespeare.* Cambridge: Harvard UP, 1973.
Based on the *Riverside Shakespeare,* this concordance, generated by computer, picks out the keywords in all the plays and poems.

Theatre Index. Twickenham, Eng.: Theatre Record, 1992–. Print.
Before 1992, this reviewing source was called the *London Theatre Index,* covering the period from 1981 to 1990. The annual resource is an index to the biweekly *Theatre Record,* which reprints newspaper and magazine reviews of current London and regional productions.

The Times Digital Archive, 1785–1985. Farmington Hills: Thomson-Gale.
Full-text and full-image articles from the *Times* of London for the years 1785–1985. It is a digital reproduction, cover to cover, of the paper in PDF files.

Ulrich's Periodical Directory. New York: Bowker, 1943– . Online and print.
Ulrich's is the most comprehensive directory and database of information about serials published worldwide. It covers journals in print, on CD-ROM, and available online as well as over five thousand daily and weekly newspapers. *Ulrich's* will indicate whether a specific journal is peer-reviewed. *Ulrichsweb.com,* the online version, is updated weekly.

Voice of the Shuttle: Web Site for Humanities Research. Apr. 2005.
Created and maintained ("woven") by Alan Liu, professor of English
at the University of California, Santa Barbara, this page is devoted
to Web sites in the humanities, including literature, literary theory,
and history.

Wellesley Index to Victorian Periodicals, 1824–1900. Toronto: U of Toronto, 1966–89.
Organized by periodical title, Wellesley indexes forty-three nineteenth-
century British periodicals. Under each title, the table of contents for
each issue is listed. This resource is also available electronically.

Index